PENGUIN CLASSICS

ON MYSTICISM

JORGE LUIS BORGES was born in Buenos Aires in 1899 and was educated in Europe. One of the most widely acclaimed writers of our time, he published many collections of poems, essays, and short stories before his death in Geneva in June 1986. In 1961, Borges shared the International Publisher's Prize with Samuel Beckett. The Ingram Merrill Foundation granted him its Annual Literary Award in 1966 for his "outstanding contribution to literature." In 1971, Columbia University awarded him the first of many degrees of Doctor of Letters, *honoris causa* (eventually the list included both Oxford and Cambridge), that he was to receive from the English-speaking world. In 1971, he also received the fifth biennial Jerusalem Prize and in 1973 was given one of Mexico's most prestigious cultural awards, the Alfonso Reyes Prize. In 1980, he shared with Gerardo Diego the Cervantes Prize, the highest literary accolade in the Spanish-speaking world. Borges was Director of the Argentine National Library from 1955 until 1973.

MARIA KODAMA is a writer, translator, and literature professor and the widow of Jorge Luis Borges. The president of Fundación Internacional Jorge Luis Borges and the heir to the Borges estate, she lives in Buenos Aires.

SUZANNE JILL LEVINE, the distinguished translator of such innovative Spanish American writers as Manuel Puig, Guillermo Cabrera Infante, Jorge Luis Borges, and Julio Cortázar, is the author of *The Subversive Scribe: Translating Latin American Fiction* and *Manuel Puig and the Spider Woman: His Life and Fictions*. A professor of Latin American literature and translation studies at the University of California at Santa Barbara, she has been awarded PEN American Center and PEN USA West awards, National Endowment for the Arts and for the Humanities grants, and a Guggenheim Foundation fellowship.

JORGE LUIS BORGES

On Mysticism

Edited with an Introduction by
MARIA KODAMA

General Editor
SUZANNE JILL LEVINE

PENGUIN BOOKS

PENGUIN BOOKS
Published by the Penguin Group
Penguin Group (USA) Inc., 375 Hudson Street, New York, New York 10014, U.S.A.
Penguin Group (Canada), 90 Eglinton Avenue East, Suite 700, Toronto, Ontario, Canada M4P 2Y3 (a division of Pearson Penguin Canada Inc.) · Penguin Books Ltd, 80 Strand, London WC2R 0RL, England · Penguin Ireland, 25 St Stephen's Green, Dublin 2, Ireland (a division of Penguin Books Ltd) · Penguin Group (Australia), 250 Camberwell Road, Camberwell, Victoria 3124, Australia (a division of Pearson Australia Group Pty Ltd) · Penguin Books India Pvt Ltd, 11 Community Centre, Panchsheel Park, New Delhi – 110 017, India · Penguin Group (NZ), 67 Apollo Drive, Rosedale, North Shore 0632, New Zealand (a division of Pearson New Zealand Ltd) · Penguin Books (South Africa) (Pty) Ltd, 24 Sturdee Avenue, Rosebank, Johannesburg 2196, South Africa

Penguin Books Ltd, Registered Offices: 80 Strand, London WC2R 0RL, England

First published in Penguin Books 2010

Grateful acknowledgment is made for permission to reprint the translations of the following works:
"Poem of the Gifts" and "Mateo, XXV: 30" translated by Alastair Reid from *Selected Poems 1923–1967* by Jorge Luis Borges, edited by Norman Thomas Di Giovanni (Delacorte Press, 1972). By permission of Alastair Reid.
"On Salvation by Deeds" from *Atlas* by Jorge Luis Borges, edited by Maria Kodama, translated by Anthony Kerrigan. Copyright © Anthony Kerrigan, 1985. Copyright © Editorial Sudamericana S.A., 1984. Used by permission of Dutton, a member of Penguin Group (USA) Inc.
"Patio" translated by Robert Fitzgerald from *Selected Poems 1923–1967* by Jorge Luis Borges, edited by Norman Thomas Di Giovanni (Delacorte Press, 1972). By permission of Penelope Laurans.

LIBRARY OF CONGRESS CATALOGING IN PUBLICATION DATA
Borges, Jorge Luis, 1899–1986.
[Selections. English. 2010]
On mysticism / Jorge Luis Borges ; edited with an introduction by Maria Kodama ; general editor, Suzanne Jill Levine.
p. cm.—(Penguin classics)
A translated collection of Borges' essays, fiction, and poetry.
Includes bibliographical references.
ISBN 978-0-14-310569-5
1. Borges, Jorge Luis, 1899–1986—Translations into English. 2. Borges, Jorge Luis, 1899–1986—Knowledge—Mysticism. 3. Borges, Jorge Luis, 1899–1986—Philosophy. I. Kodama, María. II. Levine, Suzanne Jill. III. Title.
PQ7797.B635A2 2010b
868'.62—dc22 2010011196

Set in Sabon

146086900

Contents

II. THROUGH THE LOOKING GLASS

Introduction

Jorge Luis Borges and the Mystical Experience

For me, attempting to define mysticism is like trying to explain the inexplicable. The word *mysticism* originates with the Greek mysteries, or sacred rites. A mystic was someone who had been initiated in those rites, and, as a result, had an esoteric understanding of the divine and was "eternally reborn." The ultimate goal of these initiations was to surpass the earthly world, comprising history and time, and enter into a timeless eternity. Through these mysteries, the initiate would attain something sacred, a secret wisdom of which he could not speak,

The word *mystery* comes from the Greek μυσ, which means "to close the mouth or the eyes," In Icelandic, the name *runa* comes from the verb *rymian*, which also means "mystery" and refers to something that cannot he revealed, or can only be transmitted from master to disciple. Both of these definitions refer to a hidden element that is then revealed through a transmission or initiation.

How does this connect to the idea of the mystical in the work of Jorge Luis Borges? What relation exists between the themes of time and writing?

If we refer to the Gospel, which states: "In the beginning was the Word, and the Word was with God, and the Word was God. And the Word became flesh and dwelled among us," we find ourselves facing a bifurcation of the meaning of the word *Word* across time. The path Borges chose led him to pursue the notion of the "Word" as "everything"—a concept that the poet would only be able to approach through the imperfect word.

We should also analyze the aspects that characterize mysticism. We can find similar elements in almost all the authors who specialize in this topic. First, a mystic state is ineffable; it cannot be explained or defined to someone who has not had the same experience. It is more a way of perceiving or feeling than a path deliberately taken by the intellect. Nevertheless, although the mystical state is related to a subject's emotions, it is also a state of knowledge. It is intellectual in that although such an experience cannot be expressed in words, the subject is convinced and knows for certain that he has ascended to a totally different universe—to the real universe. And though these states are brief and transitory, if the mystic follows a determined way of life he or she can experience them more frequently. St. John of the Cross affirms, "Let the soul abandon itself when it wishes to that sweet dream of love."

It is therefore possible to prepare oneself to have a mystical experience. But when one does occur, it has a passive quality to it, as if something is being given up or relinquished; the subject feels that he is lifted and sustained by a power other than his own. Another particular characteristic of a mystical state is a consciousness of the unity of everything. All creation is perceived as a unified entity. All in one and One in all. But perhaps the strangest quality of the mystical experience is the feeling of independence concerning time. The mystic captures a timeless dimension where everything assimilates to a unified essence beyond the notion of time. These states are also marked by the conviction that the ego—the I—is not real. For example, in Hinduism, the "I" that we are normally conscious of is not real; it is subject to change and deterioration. There is another entity in man: the authentic Being is the Atman, which is immortal, constant, unchanging, and is not subject to the dimensions of space and time.

Once we have determined these characteristics, we can see that they appear repeatedly in Borges's poems and short stories. I believe that we could speak, in the case of Borges, of a mysticism of creation. If the path of the mystic implies an ascetic rigor to achieve the illumination that will culminate in fusion with God, we could say that in this process Borges was detained at illumination.

Perhaps nothing awakens more compassion—in the etymological sense of the word—than that sensation of pathetic pride that belongs to agnosticism. He who believes in God affirms him and takes his experience for granted and is also equally sure of his counterpart, the atheist. However, at every moment the agnostic is attempting to understand the intangible in the only exclusively human way—through reason—which, paradoxically enough, limits him in that other dimension we have been trying to delve into. Perhaps nobody is closer to God than the agnostic.

Borges's father began teaching him philosophy as a child, and even at a very early age—in infancy—he felt a metaphysical malaise. Alongside explanations of the intractable logic of Zenon of Elea, Borges's English grandmother exposed him to the Bible. In this way, mixing reason with the Book of Books, he grew up under the sign of agnosticism, which he inherited in some way from his freethinking father.

In the epilogue *of El Hacedor* (*The Maker*) Borges writes:

> A man sets out to draw the world. As the years go by, he peoples a space with images of provinces, kingdoms, mountains, bays, ships, fish, rooms, instruments, stars, horses, and individuals. A short time before he dies, he discovers that the patient labyrinth of lines traces the lineaments of his own face.[1]

He seems to glimpse this face again in "Paradise XXXI, 108," also in *El Hacedor*: "Perhaps some feature of that crucified countenance lurks in every mirror; perhaps the face died, was obliterated, so that God could be all of us."[2]

Borges, profoundly knowledgeable of Eastern religions, here recalls Farid al-din Attar, a Persian Sufi, who "conceived the strange Simurgh (Thirty Birds)." Borges tells the story in "El Simurgh y el Águila" ("The Simurgh and the Eagle") included in *Nueve ensayos dantescos* (*Nine Dantesque Essays*). Attar was an apothecary. One afternoon a dervish entered Attar's store and told him that he must bid farewell to his possessions. Attar abandoned his store and went on a pilgrimage, finally reaching Mecca after having traveled through distant lands.

When Attar returned he dedicated himself to contemplation and writing poetry. Among the works that he left is *Mantiq al-Tayr*, the *Coloquio de los pájaros* (*The Conference of the Birds*). Toward the end of his long life, he renounced all the earthly pleasures, including versification.

The fable in Mantiq-al-Fayr tells how Simurgh, king of the birds, intentionally drops a feather in China. The birds, his subjects, decide to go in search of the feather. They know the name of their king means thirty birds and they know that he lives in the circular mountain that surrounds the earth. After crossing over oceans and valleys, only thirty reach the mountain. When they get there they realize that they are the Simurgh, that the Simurgh is each of them and all of them. The Simurgh is inextricable; he embeds pantheism.

Borges learned this story as a child and later, in *Nueve ensayos dantescos*, he compares Simurgh with the eagle that Dante describes in Canto XVIII of the *Paradiso*. Here the entire Eagle appears and is made of thousands of fair kings. However, Borges notes that the individuals that form the Eagle do not lose themselves in it. Behind the eagle Borges sees the God of Israel and of Rome, a personal god.

It's only natural that Borges would be attracted to the Sufis, given that Sufism not only produced great mystics, but also great poets. Persia could possibly be the country with the most mystical poets to be inspired by a profound spiritual experience. Christians have a mystical poet of the same stature as Attar: St. John of the Cross.

We encounter this idea again in the short story "El Aleph" ("The Aleph") from 1949. The aleph is a sphere into which the whole universe fits. Borges refers to the desperation he feels as a writer facing the impossibility of using words to describe the simultaneity that his eyes see; because the word is successive, because man is made of time, a time that is humanly successive. In this story Borges insists on the impossibility of the infinite aleph. The mystics, he says, assign emblems in an attempt to give meaning to or signify divinity. Among these emblems he mentions the Simurgh.

And with useless words he attempts to seize the vision of the unspeakable:

> I saw the Aleph from everywhere at once, saw the earth in the Aleph, saw my face and my viscera, saw your face, and I felt dizzy, and I wept, because my eyes had seen that secret, hypothetical object whose name has been usurped by men but which no man has ever truly looked upon: the inconceivable universe.[3]

We see the same idea in "El Zahir":

> In order to lose themselves in God, the Sufis repeat their own name or the ninety-nine names of God until the names mean nothing anymore. I long to travel that path. Perhaps by thinking about the Zahir unceasingly, I can manage to wear it away; perhaps behind the coin is God.[4]

Note the powerful desire expressed in the statement "I long."

The force that drags the finite conscience toward the plentitude of the infinite also compels the narrator to exclaim to Tzinacán in "La escritura del Dios" ("The Writing of the God"):

> O joy of understanding, greater than the joy of imagining, greater than the joy of feeling! [. . .] I saw the faceless god who is behind the gods. I saw the infinite processes that shape a single happiness, and, understanding all, I also came to understand the writing of the tiger.[5]

Once he has reached this revelation, nothing matters to him anymore; in understanding the universe, he knows he is nothing.

In this story, as well as in "Las ruinas circulares" ("The Circular Ruins"), Borges also explores the idea of a dream within a dream. This happens when Tzinacán dreams about the grains of sand that drown and suffocate him:

> Someone said to me: You have wakened not out of sleep, but into a prior dream, and that dream lies within another, and so

> on, to infinity, which is the number of the grains of sand. The path that you are to take is endless, and you will die before you have truly awakened.[6]

This concept that the world is a dream also references Buddhist doctrine.

Tzinacán's experience could also be framed within the beliefs and practices of Yoga; he follows a rigorous exercise involving diet, posture, breathing, intellectual concentration, and moral discipline in an attempt to unite the individual with the divine. Once the inferior nature that kept him submerged in darkness is finally defeated, man enters Samadhi and finds himself face to face with knowledge that was substantially unattainable through instinct or reason.

Citing Swami Vivenkananda's *Raja Yoga* (London 1896):

> There is no sense of the "I," but nevertheless, the mind operates independent of desire, free of the body. Truth then shines in all of its splendor and we know exactly what we are (because Samadhi potentially exists in all of us): free, immortal, omnipotent, liberated from the finite and its contrasts of good and evil. We are all one in the Atman, the Universal Spirit.

Borges, who in the "Poema de los dones" ("Poem of the Gifts") imagines Paradise in the form of the Library, went on to write "La biblioteca de Babel" ("The Library of Babel") in 1941. In this story the microcosmos is represented by the hexagons of the library's galleries—that fascinating universe "that others call the Library." Here we also see the preoccupation with finding that ultimate explanation that eludes him again and again:

> (Mystics claim that their ecstasies reveal to them a circular chamber containing an enormous circular book with a continuous spine that goes completely around the walls. But their testimony is suspect, their words obscure. That cyclical book is God.)[7]

The narrator also speaks of the Book-Man. Librarians believe that "there must exist a book that is the cipher and perfect compendium of all other books, and some librarian must have examined that book; this librarian is analogous to a god [. . .] Many have gone in search of him."[8]

Borges meditates on this double reading of the book of men and the book of nature, or the book of God, in various stories. It is impossible to approach these books with human understanding; one risks being destroyed in the attempt, like Funes the Memorious, for whom that sum of memories, the multiplicity and subtlety of differences in an insect or another animal, the infinite change from one instance to the next, only served to overwhelm him because they were already embedded in him, just as the volumes in the library of Babel were. Funes is not a mystic; through the simultaneity that he perceives he does not gain the understanding that leads to eternal harmony.

In this way, Borges's metaphysical malaise is apparent in his poems, essays, and short stories. This longing for complete and total vision compels him to plead that "in an instant, in a being, Your enormous Library find its justification."

"La biblioteca de Babel" ends with the same interminable struggle for reason to comprehend, to transgress its own limits:

> I will be bold enough to suggest this solution to the ancient problem: *The library is unlimited but periodic.* If an eternal traveler should journey in any direction, he would find after untold centuries that the same volumes are repeated in the same disorder—which, repeatedly becomes order: the Order. My solitude is cheered by that elegant hope.

As we can see, Borges's preoccupation with Order, as exposed in his justification of the Library, and in the feeling that we form part of a whole which could be God or nature, are constants that appear in different ways throughout his work. This continuous preoccupation traces his agnostic search to a moment when he had his own mystical experience.

In an interview that took place many years after it had happened, Borges recounted what he considered to be a mystical experience. He said that it lasted only a few minutes or a few seconds, adding that he couldn't be precise on how long it went on, as these things occur outside of time.

This experience is narrated in one of his first works, "El idioma de los argentinos" ("The Language of the Argentines"), from 1928, and later he included it in two more publications including "A New Refutation of Time." He referred to the experience as "sentirse en muerte," or "feeling in death":

> And here I should like to record an experience I had several nights ago: too evanescent and ecstatic a trifle to be called an adventure; too unreasonable and sentimental to be a thought. There is a scene and a word: a word I had said before but never lived with complete dedication until that night. [. . .]
>
> I remember it this way. I had spent the afternoon in Barracas, a place I rarely visited, a place whose very distance from the scene of my later wanderings gave an aura of strangeness to that day. As I had nothing to do in the evening and the weather was fair, I went out after dinner to walk and remember. I did not wish to have a set destination, I followed a random course, as much as possible; I accepted, with no conscious prejudice other than avoiding the avenues or wide streets, the most obscure invitations of chance. But a kind of familiar gravitation drew me toward certain sections I shall always remember, for they arouse in me a kind of reverence, I am not speaking of the precise environment of my childhood, my own neighborhood, but of the still mysterious fringe area beyond it, which I have possessed completely in words and but little in reality, an area that is familiar and mythological at the same time. The opposite of the known—its wrong side, so to speak—are those streets to me, almost as completely hidden as the buried foundation of our house or our invisible skeleton.
>
> The walk brought me to a corner. I breathed the night, feeling the peaceful respite from thought. The sight that greeted my eyes, uncomplicated to be sure, seemed simplified by my fatigue. Its very typicality made it unreal. The street was lined

> with low houses, and, although the first impression was poverty, the second was unsure happiness. The street was very poor and very pretty. None of the houses stood out from the rest; the fig tree cast a shadow; the doors—higher than the elongated lines of the walls—seemed to be made of the same infinite substance as the night. The footpath ran along steeply above the street, which was of elemental clay, clay of a still unconquered America. [. . .]
>
> I stood there looking at that simplicity. I thought, no doubt aloud, "This is the same as it was thirty years ago." I guessed at the date: a recent time in other countries, but already remote in this changing part of the world. Perhaps a bird was singing and I felt for him a small, bird-sized affection. What stands out most clearly; in the already vertiginous silence the only noise was the intemporal sound of the crickets. The easy thought, "I am in the eighteen hundreds" ceased to be a few careless words and deepened into reality. I felt dead—that I was an abstract perceiver of the world; I felt an undefined fear imbued with knowledge, the supreme clarity of metaphysics. No, I did not believe I had traveled across the presumptive waters of Time; rather I suspected I was the possessor of the reticent or absent meaning of the inconceivable word *eternity*. Only later was I able to define that imagining.[9]

Evidently, this experience profoundly shook his very being. He included this episode in three of his works and he recounted it again in an interview in 1977.

In some way, this seed that we see bear fruit in some of his compositions already exists in "Fervor de Buenos Aires" ("Fervor of Buenos Aires"), which as he himself said, prefigures everything that he did later. In this work, I perceive it in the poem "Un patio" ("Patio"):

> With evening
> the two or three colors of the patio grew weary.
> Tonight, the moon's bright circle,
> does not dominate outer space.
> Patio, heaven's watercourse.

The patio is the slope
down which the sky flows into the house.
Serenely
eternity waits at the crossway of the stars.
It is lovely to live in the dark friendliness
of covered entranceway, arbor, and wellhead.

The other, perhaps terrible, transcendental experience that inspired "Matthew XXV: 30" (in *El otro, el mismo* [(*The Self and the Other*], from 1964) is recalled in this verse:

"And cast ye the unprofitable servant into outer darkness: there shall be weeping and gnashing of teeth."

In his work we see that Borges knew he still had not written the poem; the poem that would trap the Word, possess the inconceivable central page—blank on its flip side—of the history of Babel, of the vision of the universe "El Aleph," and tell it without relying on linear time. With the nostalgia of his mystical experience he nevertheless knew that his redemption would be to follow his destiny and to convert the pain and joy of his earthly life into poetry. It is not in vain that he considered in "De la salvacion por las obras" ("On Salvation by Deeds") that, thanks to poetry, to a haiku, humanity was saved. Borges knew, as the pantheistic mystic Angelus Silesius said in a distich,

"The rose is without an explanation;
She blooms because she blooms."

MARIA KODAMA

NOTES

1. Andrew Hurley, translator, *Jorge Luis Borges: Collected Fictions*. (New York: Viking, 1998).
2. James E. Irby, translator, *Labyrinths: Selected Stories and Other Writing by Jorge Luis Borges*. Donald A. Yates and James E. Irby, eds. (New York: New Directions, 1964).

3. Hurley, trans., *Collected Fictions.*
4. Ibid.
5. Ibid.
6. Ibid.
7. Ibid.
8. Ibid.
9. Ruth L.C. Simms, translator, *Other Inquisitions: 1937–1952.* (Austin: University of Texas Austin Press, 1964).

A Note on the Text

Jorge Luis Borges immersed himself and his readers in metaphysical fantasies, playing reason against faith, belief systems against the methodologies of logic. He reinvented, among his many *boutades*, the ultimate metaphor of the unknowable, that symbolic structure whose center is an absence, the Labyrinth. His two principle volumes, *Ficciones* and *El Aleph*, from which several of the pieces in this collection are drawn, are filled with the games with time, space, and identity that created Borges's fame and image, and that are well represented in the first part of this volume, Borges the Mystic.

But Borges's metaphysical side also expressed itself in conversation with other thinkers, whom he engaged in essays virtually unknown to readers of English, and which are translated here for the first time. These are presented in the second part of this volume, Through the Looking Glass, and they add a new dimension to our understanding of Borges the metaphysician, for the mystical Borges evokes not one single epiphany but multiple and contradictory personae: the agnostic priest of literature, the ascetic *homo ludens*, the blind seer, the intellectual mystic, and, perhaps ultimately, the soul-seeking skeptic.

Borges was a metaphysical comedian, not unlike his esteemed Kafka, whose ultimate defense against the painful absurdity of existence was reading and writing. Literature was both prison and release, and even the loss of his eyesight could not steal its joys from him: the music of words was his most enduring religion, and he upheld this faith to his dying day. Buddhism (as Maria Kodama makes clear in her introduction to this volume) and the Kabbalah were among the religious practices from East and West that inspired Borges, and these two may also be the closest to his hermetic approach to reality's unreality. For Borges, literature was the only way to that wholeness denied to us fleeting, fragmented mortals, hence the integrity, the lucid rigor of everything he wrote.

Part II consists of five new translations by me [SJL], one in collaboration with Jessica Powell [JP]. Other translations were contributed by Esther Allen [EA], Robert Fitzgerald [RF], Andrew Hurley [AH], Anthony Kerrigan [AK], Kenneth Krabbenhoft [KK], and Alastair Reid [AR].

SUZANNE JILL LEVINE

I.

BORGES THE MYSTIC

THE CIRCULAR RUINS

And if he left off dreaming about you . . .

THROUGH THE LOOKING-GLASS, VI

No one saw him slip from the boat in the unanimous night, no one saw the bamboo canoe as it sank into the sacred mud, and yet within days there was no one who did not know that the taciturn man had come there from the South and that his homeland was one of those infinite villages that lie upriver on the violent flank of the mountain, where the language of the Zend is uncontaminated by Greek and where leprosy is uncommon. But in fact the gray man had kissed the mud, scrambled up the steep bank (without pushing back, probably without even feeling, the sharp-leaved bulrushes that slashed his flesh), and dragged himself, faint and bloody, to the circular enclosure, crowned by the stone figure of a horse or tiger, which had once been the color of fire but was now the color of ashes. That ring was a temple devoured by an ancient holocaust; now, the malarial jungle had profaned it and its god went unhonored by mankind. The foreigner lay down at the foot of the pedestal.

He was awakened by the sun high in the sky. He examined his wounds and saw, without astonishment, that they had healed; he closed his pale eyes and slept, not out of any weakness of the flesh but out of willed determination. He knew that this temple was the place that his unconquerable plan called for; he knew that the unrelenting trees had not succeeded in strangling the ruins of another promising temple downriver—like this one, a temple to dead, incinerated gods; he knew that his immediate obligation was to sleep. About midnight he was awakened by the inconsolable cry of a bird. Prints of unshod feet, a few figs, and a jug of water told him that the men of the region had respectfully spied upon his sleep and that they sought his favor, or feared his magic. He felt the coldness of fear, and he sought out a tomblike niche in the crumbling wall, where he covered himself with unknown leaves.

The goal that led him on was not impossible, though it was clearly supernatural: He wanted to dream a man. He wanted to dream him completely, in painstaking detail, and impose him upon reality. This magical objective had come to fill his entire soul; if someone had asked him his own name, or inquired into any feature of his life till then, he would not have been able to answer. The uninhabited and crumbling temple suited him, for it was a minimum of visible world; so did the proximity of the woodcutters, for they saw to his frugal needs. The rice and fruit of their tribute were nourishment enough for his body, which was consecrated to the sole task of sleeping and dreaming.

At first, his dreams were chaotic; a little later, they became dialectical. The foreigner dreamed that he was in the center of a circular amphitheater, which was somehow the ruined temple; clouds of taciturn students completely filled the terraces of seats. The faces of those farthest away hung at many centuries' distance and at a cosmic height, yet they were absolutely clear. The man lectured on anatomy, cosmography, magic; the faces listened earnestly, intently, and attempted to respond with understanding—as though they sensed the importance of that education that would redeem one of them from his state of hollow appearance and insert him into the real world. The man, both in sleep and when awake, pondered his phantasms' answers; he did not allow himself to be taken in by impostors, and he sensed in certain perplexities a growing intelligence. He was seeking a soul worthy of taking its place in the universe.

On the ninth or tenth night, he realized (with some bitterness) that nothing could be expected from those students who passively accepted his teachings, but only from those who might occasionally, in a reasonable way, venture an objection. The first—the accepting—though worthy of affection and a degree of sympathy, would never emerge as individuals; the latter—those who sometimes questioned—had a bit more preexistence. One afternoon (afternoons now paid their tribute to sleep as well; now the man was awake no more than two or three hours around daybreak) he dismissed the vast illusory classroom once and for all and retained but a single pupil—a taciturn, sallow-skinned young man, at times intractable, with sharp features that echoed those of the man that dreamed him. The pupil was not disconcerted for long by the elimination of his classmates; after only a few of the private classes, his progress amazed his teacher. Yet disaster would not be forestalled. One day the man emerged from sleep as though from a viscous desert, looked up at the hollow light of the evening (which for a moment he confused with the light of dawn), and realized that he had not dreamed. All that night and the next day, the unbearable lucidity of insomnia harried him, like a hawk. He went off to explore the jungle, hoping to tire himself; among the hemlocks he managed no more than a few intervals of feeble sleep, fleetingly veined with the most rudimentary of visions—useless to him. He reconvened his class, but no sooner had he spoken a few brief words of exhortation than the faces blurred, twisted, and faded away. In his almost perpetual state of wakefulness, tears of anger burned the man's old eyes.

He understood that the task of molding the incoherent and dizzying stuff that dreams are made of is the most difficult work a man can undertake, even if he fathom all the enigmas of the higher and lower spheres—much more difficult than weaving a rope of sand or minting coins of the faceless wind. He understood that initial failure was inevitable. He swore to put behind him the vast hallucination that at first had drawn him off the track, and he sought another way to approach his task. Before he began, he devoted a month to recovering the strength his delirium had squandered. He abandoned all premeditation of dreaming, and almost instantly managed to sleep for a fair portion of the day. The few times he did dream during this period, he did not focus on his dreams; he would wait to take up his task again until the disk of the moon was whole. Then, that evening, he purified himself in the waters of the river, bowed down to the planetary gods, uttered those syllables of a powerful name that it is lawful to pronounce, and laid himself down to sleep. Almost immediately he dreamed a beating heart.

He dreamed the heart warm, active, secret—about the size of a closed fist, a garnet-colored thing inside the dimness of a human body that was still faceless and sexless; he dreamed it, with painstaking love, for fourteen brilliant nights. Each night he perceived it with greater clarity, greater certainty. He did not touch it; he only witnessed it, observed it, corrected it, perhaps, with his eyes. He perceived it, he *lived* it, from many angles, many distances. On the fourteenth night, he stroked the pulmonary artery with his forefinger, and then the entire heart, inside and out. And his inspection made him proud. He deliberately did not sleep the next night; then he took up the heart again, invoked the name of a planet, and set about dreaming another of the major organs. Before the year was out he had reached the skeleton, the eyelids. The countless hairs of the body were perhaps the most difficult task. The man had dreamed a fully fleshed man—a stripling—but this youth did not stand up or speak, nor could it open its eyes. Night after night, the man dreamed the youth asleep.

In the cosmogonies of the Gnostics, the demiurges knead up a red Adam who cannot manage to stand; as rude and inept and elementary as that Adam of dust was the Adam of dream wrought from the sorcerer's nights. One afternoon, the man almost destroyed his creation, but he could not bring himself to do it. (He'd have been better off if he had.) After making vows to all the deities of the earth and the river, he threw himself at the feet of the idol that was perhaps a tiger or perhaps a colt, and he begged for its untried aid. That evening, at sunset, the statue filled his dreams. In the dream it was alive, and trembling—yet it was not the dread-inspiring hybrid form of horse and tiger it had been. It was, instead, those two vehement creatures plus bull, and rose, and tempest, too—and all that, simultaneously. The manifold god revealed to the man that its earthly name was Fire, and that in that circular temple (and others like it) men had made sacrifices and worshiped it, and that it would magically bring to life the phantasm the man had dreamed—so fully bring him to life that every creature, save Fire itself and the man who dreamed him, would take him for a man of flesh and blood. Fire ordered the dreamer to send the youth, once instructed in the rites, to that other ruined temple whose pyramids still stood downriver, so that a voice might glorify the god in that deserted place. In the dreaming man's dream, the dreamed man awoke.

The sorcerer carried out Fire's instructions. He consecrated a period of time (which in the end encompassed two full years) to revealing to the youth the arcana of the universe and the secrets of the cult of Fire. Deep inside, it grieved the man to separate himself from his creation. Under the pretext of pedagogical necessity, he drew out the hours of sleep more every day. He also redid the right shoulder (which was perhaps defective). From time to time, he was disturbed by a sense that all this had happened before. . . . His days were, in general, happy; when he closed his eyes, he would think *Now I will be with my son.* Or, less frequently, *The son I have engendered is waiting for me, and he will not exist if I do not go to him.*

Gradually, the man accustomed the youth to reality. Once he ordered him to set a flag on a distant mountaintop. The next day, the flag crackled on the summit. He attempted other, similar experiments—each more daring than the last. He saw with some bitterness that his son was ready—perhaps even impatient—to be born. That night he kissed him for the first time, then sent him off, through many leagues of impenetrable jungle, many leagues of swamp, to that other temple whose ruins bleached in the sun downstream. But first (so that the son would never know that he was a phantasm, so that he would believe himself to be a man like other men) the man infused in him a total lack of memory of his years of education.

The man's victory, and his peace, were dulled by the wearisome sameness of his days. In the twilight hours of dusk and dawn, he would prostrate himself before the stone figure, imagining perhaps that his unreal son performed identical rituals in other circular ruins, downstream. At night he did not dream, or dreamed the dreams that all men dream. His perceptions of the universe's sounds and shapes were somewhat pale: the absent son was nourished by those diminutions of his soul. His life's goal had been accomplished; the man lived on now in a sort of ecstasy. After a period of time (which some tellers of the story choose to compute in years, others in decades), two rowers woke the man at midnight. He could not see their faces, but they told him of a magical man in a temple in the North, a man who could walk on fire and not be burned.

The sorcerer suddenly remembered the god's words. He remembered that of all the creatures on the earth, Fire was the only one who knew that his son was a phantasm. That recollection, comforting at first, soon came to torment him. He feared that his son would meditate upon his unnatural privilege and somehow discover that he was a mere simulacrum. To be not a man, but the projection of another man's dream—what incomparable humiliation, what vertigo! Every parent feels concern for the children he has procreated (or allowed to be procreated) in happiness or in mere confusion; it was only natural that the sorcerer should fear for the future of the son he had conceived organ by organ, feature by feature, through a thousand and one secret nights.

The end of his meditations came suddenly, but it had been foretold by certain signs: first (after a long drought), a distant cloud, as light as a bird, upon a mountaintop; then, toward the South, the sky the pinkish color of a leopard's gums; then the clouds of smoke that rusted the iron of the nights; then, at last, the panicked flight of the animals—for that which had occurred hundreds of years ago was being repeated now. The ruins of the sanctuary of the god of Fire were destroyed by fire. In the birdless dawn, the sorcerer watched the concentric holocaust close in upon the walls. For a moment he thought of taking refuge in the water, but then he realized that death would be a crown upon his age and absolve him from his labors. He walked into the tatters of flame, but they did not bite his flesh—they caressed him, bathed him without heat and without combustion. With relief, with humiliation, with terror, he realized that he, too, was but appearance, that another man was dreaming him.

[1941] *[AH]*

THE LIBRARY OF BABEL

By this art you may contemplate the variation of the 23 letters. . . .

ANATOMY OF MELANCHOLY, PT. 2, SEC. II, MEM. IV

The universe (which others call the Library) is composed of an indefinite, perhaps infinite number of hexagonal galleries. In the center of each gallery is a ventilation shaft, bounded by a low railing. From any hexagon one can see the floors above and below—one after another, endlessly. The arrangement of the galleries is always the same: Twenty bookshelves, five to each side, line four of the hexagon's six sides; the height of the bookshelves, floor to ceiling, is hardly greater than the height of a normal librarian. One of the hexagons free sides opens onto a narrow sort of vestibule, which in turn opens onto another gallery, identical to the first—identical in fact to all. To the left and right of the vestibule are two tiny compartments. One is for sleeping, upright; the other, for satisfying one's physical necessities. Through this space, too, there passes a spiral staircase, which winds upward and downward into the remotest distance. In the vestibule there is a mirror, which faithfully duplicates appearances. Men often infer from this mirror that the Library is not infinite—if it were, what need would there be for that illusory replication? I prefer to dream that burnished surfaces are a figuration and promise of the infinite. . . . Light is provided by certain spherical fruits that bear the name "bulbs." There are two of these bulbs in each hexagon, set crosswise. The light they give is insufficient, and unceasing.

Like all the men of the Library, in my younger days I traveled; I have journeyed in quest of a book, perhaps the catalog of catalogs. Now that my eyes can hardly make out what I myself have written, I am preparing to die, a few leagues from the hexagon where I was born. When I am dead, compassionate hands will throw me over the railing; my tomb will be the unfathomable air, my body will sink for ages, and will decay and dissolve in the wind engendered by my fall, which shall be infinite. I declare that the Library is endless. Idealists argue that the hexagonal rooms are the necessary shape of absolute space, or at least of our *perception* of space. They argue that a triangular or pentagonal chamber is inconceivable. (Mystics claim that their ecstasies reveal to them a circular chamber containing an enormous circular book with a continuous spine that goes completely around the walls. But their testimony is suspect, their words obscure. That cyclical book is God.) Let it suffice for the moment that I repeat the classic dictum: *The Library is a sphere whose exact center is any hexagon and whose circumference is unattainable.*

Each wall of each hexagon is furnished with five bookshelves; each bookshelf holds thirty-two books identical in format; each book contains four hundred ten pages; each page, forty lines; each line, approximately eighty black letters. There are also letters on the front cover of each book; those letters neither indicate nor prefigure what the pages inside will say. I am aware that that lack of correspondence once struck men as mysterious. Before summarizing the solution of the mystery (whose discovery, in spite of its tragic consequences, is perhaps the most important event in all history), I wish to recall a few axioms.

First: *The Library has existed* ab æternitate. That truth, whose immediate corollary is the future eternity of the world, no rational mind can doubt. Man, the imperfect librarian, may be the work of chance or of malevolent demiurges; the universe, with its elegant appointments—its bookshelves, its enigmatic books, its indefatigable staircases for the traveler, and its water closets for the seated librarian—can only be the handiwork of a god. In order to grasp the distance that separates the human and the divine, one has only to compare these crude trembling symbols which my fallible hand scrawls on the cover of a book with the organic letters inside—neat, delicate, deep black, and inimitably symmetrical.

Second: *There are twenty-five orthographic symbols.*[1] That discovery enabled mankind, three hundred years ago, to formulate a general theory of the Library and thereby satisfactorily solve the riddle that no conjecture had been able to divine—the formless and chaotic nature of virtually all books. One book, which my father once saw in a hexagon in circuit 15-94, consisted of the letters M C V perversely repeated from the first line to the last. Another (much consulted in this zone) is a mere labyrinth of letters whose penultimate page contains the phrase *O Time thy pyramids*. This much is known: For every rational line or forthright statement there are leagues of senseless cacophony, verbal nonsense, and incoherency. (I know of one semibarbarous zone whose librarians repudiate the "vain and superstitious habit" of trying to find sense in books, equating such a quest with attempting to find meaning in dreams or in the chaotic lines of the palm of one's hand. . . . They will acknowledge that the inventors of writing imitated the twenty-five natural symbols, but contend that that adoption was fortuitous, coincidental, and that books in themselves have no meaning. That argument, as we shall see, is not entirely fallacious.)

For many years it was believed that those impenetrable books were in ancient or far-distant languages. It is true that the most ancient peoples, the first librarians, employed a language quite different from the one we speak today; it is true that a few miles to the right, our language devolves into dialect and that ninety floors above, it becomes incomprehensible. All of that, I repeat, is true—but four hundred ten pages of unvary-

1 The original manuscript has neither numbers nor capital letters; punctuation is limited to the comma and the period. Those two marks, the space, and the twenty-two letters of the alphabet are the twenty-five sufficient symbols that our unknown author is referring to. [Ed. note.]

ing M C V's cannot belong to any language, however dialectal or primitive it may be. Some have suggested that each letter influences the next, and that the value of M C V on page 71, line 3, is not the value of the same series on another line of another page, but that vague thesis has not met with any great acceptance. Others have mentioned the possibility of codes; that conjecture has been universally accepted, though not in the sense in which its originators formulated it.

Some five hundred years ago, the chief of one of the upper hexagons[2] came across a book as jumbled as all the others, but containing almost two pages of homogeneous lines. He showed his find to a traveling decipherer, who told him that the lines were written in Portuguese; others said it was Yiddish. Within the century experts had determined what the language actually was: a Samoyed-Lithuanian dialect of Guarani, with inflections from classical Arabic. The content was also determined: the rudiments of combinatory analysis, illustrated with examples of endlessly repeating variations. Those examples allowed a librarian of genius to discover the fundamental law of the Library. This philosopher observed that all books, however different from one another they might be, consist of identical elements: the space, the period, the comma, and the twenty-two letters of the alphabet. He also posited a fact which all travelers have since confirmed: *In all the Library, there are no two identical books*. From those incontrovertible premises, the librarian deduced that the Library is "total"—perfect, complete, and whole—and that its bookshelves contain all possible combinations of the twenty-two orthographic symbols (a number which, though unimaginably vast, is not infinite)—that is, all that is able to be expressed, in every language. *All*—the detailed history of the future, the autobiographies of the archangels, the faithful catalog of the Library, thousands and thousands of false catalogs, the proof of the falsity of those false catalogs, a proof of the falsity of the *true* catalog, the gnostic gospel of

2 In earlier times, there was one man for every three hexagons. Suicide and diseases of the lung have played havoc with that proportion. An unspeakably melancholy memory: I have sometimes traveled for nights on end, down corridors and polished staircases, without coming across a single librarian.

Basilides, the commentary upon that gospel, the commentary on the commentary on that gospel, the true story of your death, the translation of every book into every language, the interpolations of every book into all books, the treatise Bede could have written (but did not) on the mythology of the Saxon people, the lost books of Tacitus.

When it was announced that the Library contained all books, the first reaction was unbounded joy. All men felt themselves the possessors of an intact and secret treasure. There was no personal problem, no world problem, whose eloquent solution did not exist—somewhere in some hexagon. The universe was justified; the universe suddenly became congruent with the unlimited width and breadth of humankind's hope. At that period there was much talk of The Vindications—books of *apologiæ* and prophecies that would vindicate for all time the actions of every person in the universe and that held wondrous arcana for men's futures. Thousands of greedy individuals abandoned their sweet native hexagons and rushed downstairs, upstairs, spurred by the vain desire to find their Vindication. These pilgrims squabbled in the narrow corridors, muttered dark imprecations, strangled one another on the divine staircases, threw deceiving volumes down ventilation shafts, were themselves hurled to their deaths by men of distant regions. Others went insane. . . . The Vindications do exist (I have seen two of them, which refer to persons in the future, persons perhaps not imaginary), but those who went in quest of them failed to recall that the chance of a man's finding his own Vindication, or some perfidious version of his own, can be calculated to be zero.

At that same period there was also hope that the fundamental mysteries of mankind—the origin of the Library and of time—might be revealed. In all likelihood those profound mysteries can indeed be explained in words; if the language of the philosophers is not sufficient, then the multiform Library must surely have produced the extraordinary language that is required, together with the words and grammar of that language. For four centuries, men have been scouring the hexagons. . . . There are official searchers, the "inquisitors." I have seen them about their tasks: they arrive exhausted at some hexagon, they talk about a staircase that nearly killed them—some steps were missing—they speak with the librarian about galleries and staircases, and, once in a while, they take up the nearest book and leaf through it, searching for disgraceful or dishonorable words. Clearly, no one expects to discover anything.

That unbridled hopefulness was succeeded, naturally enough, by a similarly disproportionate depression. The certainty that some bookshelf in some hexagon contained precious books, yet that those precious books were forever out of reach, was almost unbearable. One blasphemous sect proposed that the searches be discontinued and that all men shuffle letters and symbols until those canonical books, through some improbable stroke of chance, had been constructed. The authorities were forced to issue strict orders. The sect disappeared, but in my childhood I have seen old men who for long periods would hide in the latrines with metal disks and a forbidden dice cup, feebly mimicking the divine disorder.

Others, going about it in the opposite way, thought the first thing to do was eliminate all worthless books. They would invade the hexagons, show credentials that were not always false, leaf disgustedly through a volume, and condemn entire walls of books. It is to their hygienic, ascetic rage that we lay the senseless loss of millions of volumes. Their name is execrated today, but those who grieve over the "treasures" destroyed in that frenzy overlook two widely acknowledged facts: One, that the Library is so huge that any reduction by human hands must be infinitesimal. And two, that each book is unique and irreplaceable, but (since the Library is total) there are always several hundred thousand imperfect facsimiles—books that differ by no more than a single letter, or a comma. Despite general opinion, I daresay that the consequences of the depredations committed by the Purifiers have been exaggerated by the horror those same fanatics inspired. They were spurred on by the holy zeal to reach—someday, through unrelenting effort—the books of the Crimson Hexagon—books smaller than natural books, books omnipotent, illustrated, and magical.

We also have knowledge of another superstition from that

period: belief in what was termed the Book-Man. On some shelf in some hexagon, it was argued, there must exist a book that is the cipher and perfect compendium *of all other books*, and some librarian must have examined that book; this librarian is analogous to a god. In the language of this zone there are still vestiges of the sect that worshiped that distant librarian. Many have gone in search of Him. For a hundred years, men beat every possible path—and every path in vain. How was one to locate the idolized secret hexagon that sheltered Him? Someone proposed searching by regression: To locate book A, first consult book B, which tells where book A can be found; to locate book B, first consult book C, and so on, to infinity. . . . It is in ventures such as these that I have squandered and spent my years. I cannot think it unlikely that there is such a total book[3] on some shelf in the universe. I pray to the unknown gods that some man—even a single man, tens of centuries ago—has perused and read that book. If the honor and wisdom and joy of such a reading are not to be my own, then let them be for others. Let heaven exist, though my own place be in hell. Let me be tortured and battered and annihilated, but let there be one instant, one creature, wherein thy enormous Library may find its justification.

Infidels claim that the rule in the Library is not "sense," but "non-sense," and that "rationality" (even humble, pure coherence) is an almost miraculous exception. They speak, I know, of "the feverish Library, whose random volumes constantly threaten to transmogrify into others, so that they affirm all things, deny all things, and confound and confuse all things, like some mad and hallucinating deity." Those words, which not only proclaim disorder but exemplify it as well, prove, as all can see, the infidels' deplorable taste and desperate ignorance. For while the Library contains all verbal structures, all the variations allowed by the twenty-five orthographic symbols, it includes not a single absolute piece of

3 I repeat: In order for a book to exist, it is sufficient that it be *possible*. Only the impossible is excluded. For example, no book is also a staircase, though there are no doubt books that discuss and deny and prove that possibility, and others whose structure corresponds to that of a staircase.

nonsense. It would be pointless to observe that the finest volume of all the many hexagons that I myself administer is titled *Combed Thunder*, while another is titled *The Plaster Cramp*, and another, *Axaxaxas mlö*. Those phrases, at first apparently incoherent, are undoubtedly susceptible to cryptographic or allegorical "reading"; that reading, that justification of the words' order and existence, is itself verbal and, *ex hypothesi*, already contained somewhere in the Library. There is no combination of characters one can make—*dhcmrlchtdj*, for example—that the divine Library has not foreseen and that in one or more of its secret tongues does not hide a terrible significance. There is no syllable one can speak that is not filled with tenderness and terror, that is not, in one of those languages, the mighty name of a god. To speak is to commit tautologies. This pointless, verbose epistle already exists in one of the thirty volumes of the five bookshelves in one of the countless hexagons—as does its refutation. (A number *n* of the possible languages employ the same vocabulary; in some of them, the *symbol* "library" possesses the correct definition "everlasting, ubiquitous system of hexagonal galleries," while a library—the thing—is a loaf of bread or a pyramid or something else, and the six words that define it themselves have other definitions. You who read me—are you certain you understand my language?)

Methodical composition distracts me from the present condition of humanity. The certainty that everything has already been written annuls us, or renders us phantasmal. I know districts in which the young people prostrate themselves before books and like savages kiss their pages, though they cannot read a letter. Epidemics, heretical discords, pilgrimages that inevitably degenerate into brigandage have decimated the population. I believe I mentioned the suicides, which are more and more frequent every year. I am perhaps misled by old age and fear, but I suspect that the human species—the *only* species—teeters at the verge of extinction, yet that the Library—enlightened, solitary, infinite, perfectly unmoving, armed with precious volumes, pointless, incorruptible, and secret—will endure.

I have just written the word "infinite." I have not included that adjective out of mere rhetorical habit; I hereby state that it is not illogical to think that the world is infinite. Those who believe it to have limits hypothesize that in some remote place or places the corridors and staircases and hexagons may, inconceivably, end—which is absurd. And yet those who picture the world as unlimited forget that the number of possible books is *not*. I will be bold enough to suggest this solution to the ancient problem: *The Library is unlimited but periodic*. If an eternal traveler should journey in any direction, he would find after untold centuries that the same volumes are repeated in the same disorder—which, repeated, becomes order: the Order. My solitude is cheered by that elegant hope.[4]

Mar del Plata, 1941

[*1941*] [*AH*]

4 Letizia Alvarez de Toledo has observed that the vast Library is pointless; strictly speaking, all that is required is *a single volume*, of the common size, printed in nine- or ten-point type, that would consist of an infinite number of infinitely thin pages. (In the early seventeenth century, Cavalieri stated that every solid body is the superposition of an infinite number of planes.) Using that silken *vademecum* would not be easy: each apparent page would open into other similar pages; the inconceivable middle page would have no "back."

FUNES THE MEMORIOUS

I recall him (though I have no right to speak that sacred verb—only one man on earth did, and that man is dead) holding a dark passionflower in his hand, seeing it as it had never been seen, even had it been stared at from the first light of dawn till the last light of evening for an entire lifetime. I recall him—his taciturn face, its Indian features, its extraordinary *remoteness*—behind the cigarette. I recall (I think) the slender, leather-braider's fingers. I recall near those hands a *mate* cup, with the coat of arms of the Banda Oriental. I recall, in the window of his house, a yellow straw blind with some vague painted lake scene. I clearly recall his voice—the slow, resentful, nasal voice of the toughs of those days, without the Italian sibilants one hears today. I saw him no more than three times, the last time in 1887. . . . I applaud the idea that all of us who had dealings with the man should write something about him; my testimony will perhaps be the briefest (and certainly the slightest) account in the volume that you are to publish, but it can hardly be the least impartial. Unfortunately I am Argentine, and so congenitally unable to produce the dithyramb that is the obligatory genre in Uruguay, especially when the subject is an Uruguayan. *Highbrow, dandy, city slicker*—Funes did not utter those insulting words, but I know with reasonable certainty that to him I represented those misfortunes. Pedro Leandro Ipuche has written that Funes was a precursor of the race of supermen—"a maverick and vernacular Zarathustra"—and I will not argue the point, but one must not forget that he was also a street tough from Fray Bentos, with certain incorrigible limitations.

My first recollection of Funes is quite clear. I see him one afternoon in March or February of '84. That year, my father had taken me to spend the summer in Fray Bentos. I was coming back from the ranch in San Francisco with my cousin Bernardo Haedo. We were riding along on our horses, singing merrily—and being on horseback was not the only reason for my cheerfulness. After a sultry day, a huge slate-colored storm, fanned by the south wind, had curtained the sky. The wind flailed the trees wildly, and I was filled with the fear (the hope) that we would be surprised in the open countryside by the elemental water. We ran a kind of race against the storm. We turned into the deep bed of a narrow street that ran between two brick sidewalks built high up off the ground. It had suddenly got dark; I heard quick, almost secret footsteps above me—I raised my eyes and saw a boy running along the narrow, broken sidewalk high above, as though running along the top of a narrow, broken wall. I recall the short, baggy trousers—like a gaucho's—that he wore, the straw-soled cotton slippers, the cigarette in the hard visage, all stark against the now limitless storm cloud. Unexpectedly, Bernardo shouted out to him—*What's the time, Ireneo?* Without consulting the sky, without a second's pause, the boy replied, *Four minutes till eight, young Bernardo Juan Francisco.* The voice was shrill and mocking.

I am so absentminded that I would never have given a second thought to the exchange I've just reported had my attention not been called to it by my cousin, who was prompted by a certain local pride and the desire to seem unfazed by the other boy's trinomial response.

He told me that the boy in the narrow street was one Ireneo Funes, and that he was known for certain eccentricities, among them shying away from people and always knowing what time it was, like a clock. He added that Ireneo was the son of a village ironing woman, María Clementina Funes, and that while some people said his father was a doctor in the salting house (an Englishman named O'Connor), others said he broke horses or drove oxcarts for a living over in the department of Salto. The boy lived with his mother, my cousin told me, around the corner from Villa Los Laureles.

In '85 and '86, we spent the summer in Montevideo; it was

not until '87 that I returned to Fray Bentos. Naturally, I asked about everybody I knew, and finally about "chronometric Funes." I was told he'd been bucked off a half-broken horse on the ranch in San Francisco and had been left hopelessly crippled. I recall the sensation of unsettling magic that this news gave me: The only time I'd seen him, we'd been coming home on horseback from the ranch in San Francisco, and he had been walking along a high place. This new event, told by my cousin Bernardo, struck me as very much like a dream confected out of elements of the past. I was told that Funes never stirred from his cot, his eyes fixed on the fig tree behind the house or on a spiderweb. At dusk, he would let himself be carried to the window. He was such a proud young man that he pretended that his disastrous fall had actually been fortunate. . . . Twice I saw him, on his cot behind the iron-barred window that crudely underscored his prisonerlike state—once lying motionless, with his eyes closed; the second time motionless as well, absorbed in the contemplation of a fragrant switch of artemisia.

It was not without some self-importance that about that same time I had embarked upon a systematic study of Latin. In my suitcase I had brought with me Lhomond's *De viris illustribus*, Quicherat's *Thesaurus*, Julius Caesar's commentaries, and an odd-numbered volume of Pliny's *Naturalis historia*—a work which exceeded (and still exceeds) my modest abilities as a Latinist. There are no secrets in a small town; Ireneo, in his house on the outskirts of the town, soon learned of the arrival of those outlandish books. He sent me a flowery, sententious letter, reminding me of our "lamentably ephemeral" meeting "on the seventh of February, 1884." He dwelt briefly, elegiacally, on the "glorious services" that my uncle, Gregorio Haedo, who had died that same year, "had rendered to his two motherlands in the valiant Battle of Ituzaingó," and then he begged that I lend him one of the books I had brought, along with a dictionary "for a full understanding of the text, since I must plead ignorance of Latin." He promised to return the books to me in good condition, and "straightway." The penmanship was perfect, the letters exceptionally well formed; the spelling was that recommended by Andrés Bello: *i* for *y*, *j* for *g*. At first, of course, I thought it was some sort of joke. My cousins assured me it was not, that this "was just . . . just Ireneo." I didn't know whether to attribute to brazen conceit, ignorance, or stupidity the idea that hard-won Latin needed no more teaching than a dictionary could give; in order to fully disabuse Funes, I sent him Quicherat's *Gradus ad Parnassum* and the Pliny.

On February 14, I received a telegram from Buenos Aires urging me to return home immediately; my father was "not at all well." God forgive me, but the prestige of being the recipient of an urgent telegram, the desire to communicate to all of Fray Bentos the contradiction between the negative form of the news and the absoluteness of the adverbial phrase, the temptation to dramatize my grief by feigning a virile stoicism—all this perhaps distracted me from any possibility of real pain. As I packed my bag, I realized that I didn't have the *Gradus ad Parnassum* and the first volume of Pliny. The *Saturn* was to sail the next morning; that evening, after dinner, I walked over to Funes' house. I was amazed that the evening was no less oppressive than the day had been.

At the honest little house, Funes' mother opened the door.

She told me that Ireneo was in the back room. I shouldn't be surprised if I found the room dark, she told me, since Ireneo often spent his off hours without lighting the candle. I walked across the tiled patio and down the little hallway farther on, and came to the second patio. There was a grapevine; the darkness seemed to me virtually total. Then suddenly I heard Ireneo's high, mocking voice. The voice was speaking Latin; with morbid pleasure, the voice emerging from the shadows was reciting a speech or a prayer or an incantation. The Roman syllables echoed in the patio of hard-packed earth; my trepidation made me think them incomprehensible, and endless; later, during the enormous conversation of that night, I learned they were the first paragraph of the twenty-fourth chapter of the seventh book of Pliny's *Naturalis historia*. The subject of that chapter is memory; the last words were *ut nihil non iisdem verbis redderetur auditum*.

Without the slightest change of voice, Ireneo told me to come in. He was lying on his cot, smoking. I don't think I saw his face until the sun came up the next morning; when I look back, I believe I recall the momentary glow of his cigarette. His room smelled vaguely musty. I sat down; I told him about my telegram and my father's illness.

I come now to the most difficult point in my story, a story whose only *raison d'être* (as my readers should be told from the outset) is that dialogue half a century ago. I will not attempt to reproduce the words of it, which are now forever irrecoverable. Instead, I will summarize, faithfully, the many things Ireneo told me. Indirect discourse is distant and weak; I know that I am sacrificing the effectiveness of my tale. I only ask that my readers try to hear in their imagination the broken and staccato periods that astounded me that night.

Ireneo began by enumerating, in both Latin and Spanish, the cases of prodigious memory cataloged in the *Naturalis historia*: Cyrus, the king of Persia, who could call all the soldiers in his armies by name; Mithridates Eupator, who meted out justice in the twenty-two languages of the kingdom over which he ruled; Simonides, the inventor of the art of memory; Metrodorus, who was able faithfully to repeat what he had heard, though it be but once. With obvious sincerity, Ireneo said he was amazed that such cases were thought to be amazing. He told me that before that rainy afternoon when the blue roan had bucked him off, he had been what every man was—blind, deaf, befuddled, and virtually devoid of memory. (I tried to remind him how precise his perception of time, his memory for proper names had been—he ignored me.) He had lived, he said, for nineteen years as though in a dream: he looked without seeing, heard without listening, forgot everything, or virtually everything. When he fell, he'd been knocked unconscious; when he came to again, the present was so rich, so clear, that it was almost unbearable, as were his oldest and even his most trivial memories. It was shortly afterward that he learned he was crippled; of that fact he hardly took notice. He reasoned (or felt) that immobility was a small price to pay. Now his perception and his memory were perfect.

With one quick look, you and I perceive three wineglasses on a table; Funes perceived every grape that had been pressed into the wine and all the stalks and tendrils of its vineyard. He knew the forms of the clouds in the southern sky on the morning of April 30, 1882, and he could compare them in his memory with the veins in the marbled binding of a book he had seen only once, or with the feathers of spray lifted by an oar on the Rio Negro on the eve of the Battle of Quebracho. Nor were those memories simple—every visual image was linked to muscular sensations, thermal sensations, and so on. He was able to reconstruct every dream, every daydream he had ever had. Two or three times he had reconstructed an entire day; he had never once erred or faltered, but each reconstruction had itself taken an entire day. "*I, myself, alone, have more memories than all mankind since the world began,*" he said to me. And also: "*My dreams are like other people's waking hours.*" And again, toward dawn: "*My memory, sir, is like a garbage heap.*" A circle drawn on a blackboard, a right triangle, a rhombus—all these are forms we can fully intuit; Ireneo could do the same with the stormy mane of a young colt, a small herd of cattle on a mountainside, a flickering fire and its uncountable ashes, and the many faces of a dead man at a wake. I have no idea how many stars he saw in the sky.

Those are the things he told me; neither then nor later have I ever doubted them. At that time there were no cinematographers, no phonographs; it nevertheless strikes me as implausible, even incredible, that no one ever performed an experiment with Funes. But then, all our lives we postpone everything that can be postponed; perhaps we all have the certainty, deep inside, that we are immortal and that sooner or later every man will do everything, know all there is to know.

The voice of Funes, from the darkness, went on talking.

He told me that in 1886 he had invented a numbering system original with himself, and that within a very few days he had passed the twenty-four thousand mark. He had not written it down, since anything he thought, even once, remained ineradicably with him. His original motivation, I think, was his irritation that the thirty-three Uruguayan patriots should require two figures and three words rather than a single figure, a single word. He then applied this mad principle to the other numbers. Instead of seven thousand thirteen (7013), he would say, for instance, "Maxímo Pérez"; instead of seven thousand fourteen (7014), "the railroad"; other numbers were "Luis Melián Lafinur," "Olimar," "sulfur," "clubs," "the whale," "gas," "a stewpot," "Napoleon," "Agustín de Vedia." Instead of five hundred (500), he said "nine." Every word had a particular figure attached to it, a sort of marker; the later ones were extremely complicated. . . . I tried to explain to Funes that his rhapsody of unconnected words was exactly the opposite of a number *system*. I told him that when one said "365" one said "three hundreds, six tens, and five ones," a breakdown impossible with the "numbers" *Nigger Timoteo* or *a ponchoful of meat*. Funes either could not or would not understand me.

In the seventeenth century, Locke postulated (and condemned) an impossible language in which each individual thing—every stone, every bird, every branch—would have its own name; Funes once contemplated a similar language, but discarded the idea as too general, too ambiguous. The truth was, Funes remembered not only every leaf of every tree in every patch of forest, but every time he had perceived or imagined that leaf. He resolved to reduce every one of his past days to some seventy thousand recollections, which he would then define by numbers. Two considerations dissuaded him: the realization that the task was interminable, and the realization that it was pointless. He saw that by the time he died he would still not have finished classifying all the memories of his childhood.

The two projects I have mentioned (an infinite vocabulary for the natural series of numbers, and a pointless mental catalog of all the images of his memory) are foolish, even preposterous, but they reveal a certain halting grandeur. They allow us to glimpse, or to infer, the dizzying world that Funes lived in. Funes, we must not forget, was virtually incapable of general, platonic ideas. Not only was it difficult for him to see that the generic symbol "dog" took in all the dissimilar individuals of all shapes and sizes, it irritated him that the "dog" of three-fourteen in the afternoon, seen in profile, should be indicated by the same noun as the dog of three-fifteen, seen frontally. His own face in the mirror, his own hands, surprised him every time he saw them. Swift wrote that the emperor of Lilliput could perceive the movement of the minute hand of a clock; Funes could continually perceive the quiet advances of corruption, of tooth decay, of weariness. He saw—he *noticed*—the progress of death, of humidity. He was the solitary, lucid spectator of a multiform, momentaneous, and almost unbearably precise world. Babylon, London, and New York dazzle mankind's imagination with their fierce splendor; no one in the populous towers or urgent avenues of those cities has ever felt the heat and pressure of a reality as inexhaustible as that which battered Ireneo, day and night, in his poor South American hinterland. It was hard for him to sleep. To sleep is to take one's mind from the world; Funes, lying on his back on his cot, in the dimness of his room, could picture every crack in the wall, every molding of the precise houses that surrounded him. (I repeat that the most trivial of his memories was more detailed, more vivid than our own perception of a physical pleasure or a physical torment.) Off toward the east, in an area that had not yet been cut up into city blocks, there were new houses, unfamiliar to Ireneo. He pictured them to himself as black, compact, made of homogeneous shadow; he would turn his head in that direction to sleep. He would also imagine himself at the bottom of a river, rocked (and negated) by the current.

He had effortlessly learned English, French, Portuguese, Latin. I suspect, nevertheless, that he was not very good at thinking. To think is to ignore (or forget) differences, to generalize, to abstract. In the teeming world of Ireneo Funes there was nothing but particulars—and they were virtually *immediate* particulars.

The leery light of dawn entered the patio of packed earth.

It was then that I saw the face that belonged to the voice that had been talking all night long. Ireneo was nineteen, he had been born in 1868; he looked to me as monumental as bronze—older than Egypt, older than the prophecies and the pyramids. I was struck by the thought that every word I spoke, every expression of my face or motion of my hand would endure in his implacable memory; I was rendered clumsy by the fear of making pointless gestures.

Ireneo Funes died in 1889 of pulmonary congestion.

[*1942*] [*AH*]

THE ALEPH

O God, I could be bounded in a nutshell and count myself a King of infinite space.

HAMLET, II:2

But they will teach us that Eternity is the Standing still of the Present Time, a *Nunc-stans* (as the Schools call it); which neither they, nor any else understand, no more than they would a *Hic-stans* for an Infinite greatnesse of Place.

LEVIATHAN, IV:46

That same sweltering February morning that Beatriz Viterbo died, after an imperious confrontation with her illness in which she had never for an instant stooped to either sentimentality or fear, I noticed that a new advertisement for some cigarettes or other (*blondes*, I believe they were) had been posted on the iron billboards of the Plaza Constitución; the fact deeply grieved me, for I realized that the vast unceasing universe was already growing away from her, and that this change was but the first in an infinite series. *The universe may change, but I shall not*, thought I with melancholy vanity. I knew that more than once my futile devotion had exasperated her; now that she was dead, I could consecrate myself to her memory—without hope, but also without humiliation. I reflected that April 30 was her birthday; stopping by her house on Calle Garay that day to pay my respects to her father and her first cousin Carlos Argentino Daneri was an irreproachable, perhaps essential act of courtesy. Once again I would wait in the half-light of the little parlor crowded with furniture and draperies and bric-a-brac, once again I would study the details of the many photographs and portraits of her: Beatriz Viterbo, in profile, in color; Beatriz in a mask at the Carnival of 1921; Beatriz' first communion; Beatriz on the day of her wedding to Roberto Alessandri; Beatriz shortly after the divorce, lunching at the Jockey Club; Beatriz in Quilmes with Delia San Marco Porcel and Carlos Argentino; Beatriz with the Pekinese that had been a gift from Villegas Haedo; Beatriz in full-front and in three-quarters view, smiling, her hand on her chin. . . . I would not be obliged, as I had been on occasions before, to justify my presence with modest offerings of books—books whose pages I learned at last to cut, so as not to find, months later, that they were still intact.

Beatriz Viterbo died in 1929; since then, I have not allowed an April 30 to pass without returning to her house. That first time, I arrived at seven-fifteen and stayed for about twenty-five minutes; each year I would turn up a little later and stay a little longer; in 1933, a downpour came to my aid: they were forced to ask me to dinner. Naturally, I did not let that fine precedent go to waste; in 1934 I turned up a few minutes after eight with a lovely confection from Santa Fe; it was perfectly natural that I should stay for dinner. And so it was that on those melancholy and vainly erotic anniversaries I came to receive the gradual confidences of Carlos Argentino Daneri.

Beatriz was tall, fragile, very slightly stooped; in her walk, there was (if I may be pardoned the oxymoron) something of a graceful clumsiness, a *soupçon* of hesitancy, or of palsy; Carlos Argentino is a pink, substantial, gray-haired man of refined features. He holds some sort of subordinate position in an illegible library in the outskirts toward the south of the city; he is authoritarian, though also ineffectual; until very recently he took advantage of nights and holidays to remain at home. At two generations' remove, the Italian *s* and the liberal Italian gesticulation still survive in him. His mental activity is constant, passionate, versatile, and utterly insignificant. He is full of pointless analogies and idle scruples. He has (as Beatriz did) large, beautiful, slender hands. For some months he labored under an obsession for Paul Fort, less for Fort's ballads than the idea of a glory that could never be tarnished. "He is the prince of the poets of *la belle France*," he would fatuously say. "You assail him in vain; you shall never touch him—not even the most venomous of your darts shall ever touch him."

On April 30, 1941, I took the liberty of enriching my sweet offering with a bottle of domestic brandy. Carlos Argentino tasted it, pronounced it "interesting," and, after a few snifters, launched into a vindication of modern man.

"I picture him," he said with an animation that was rather unaccountable, "in his study, as though in the watchtower of a great city, surrounded by telephones, telegraphs, phonographs, the latest in radio-telephone and motion-picture and magic-lantern equipment, and glossaries and calendars and timetables and bulletins. . . ."

He observed that for a man so equipped, the act of traveling was supererogatory; this twentieth century of ours had upended the fable of Muhammad and the mountain—mountains nowadays did in fact come to the modern Muhammad.

So witless did these ideas strike me as being, so sweeping and pompous the way they were expressed, that I associated them immediately with literature. Why, I asked him, didn't he write these ideas down? Predictably, he replied that he already had; they, and others no less novel, figured large in the Augural Canto, Prologurial Canto, or simply Prologue-Canto, of a poem on which he had been working, with no deafening hurly-burly and *sans réclame*, for many years, leaning always on those twin staffs Work and Solitude. First he would open the floodgates of the imagination, then repair to the polishing wheel. The poem was entitled *The Earth*; it centered on a description of our own terraqueous orb and was graced, of course, with picturesque digression and elegant apostrophe.

I begged him to read me a passage, even if only a brief one. He opened a desk drawer, took out a tall stack of tablet paper stamped with the letterhead of the Juan Crisóstomo Lafinur Library, and read, with ringing self-satisfaction:

I have seen, as did the Greek, man's cities and his fame,
The works, the days of various light, the hunger;
I prettify no fact, I falsify no name,
For the voyage I narrate is . . . *autour de ma chambre.*

"A stanza interesting from every point of view," he said. "The first line wins the kudos of the learned, the academician, the Hellenist—though perhaps not that of those would-be scholars that make up such a substantial portion of popular opinion. The second moves from Homer to Hesiod (implicit homage, at the very threshold of the dazzling new edifice, to the father of didactic poetry), not without revitalizing a technique whose lineage may be traced to Scripture—that is, enumeration, congeries, or conglobation. The third—baroque? decadent? the purified and fanatical cult of form?—consists of twinned hemistichs; the fourth, unabashedly bilingual, assures me the unconditional support of every spirit able to feel the ample attractions of playfulness. I shall say nothing of the unusual rhyme, nor of the erudition that allows me—without pedantry or boorishness!—to include within the space of four lines three erudite allusions spanning thirty centuries of dense literature: first the *Odyssey*, second the *Works and Days*, and third that immortal bagatelle that regales us with the diversions of the Savoyard's plume. . . . Once again, I show my awareness that truly *modern* art demands the balm of laughter, of scherzo. There is no doubt about it—Goldoni was right!"

Carlos Argentino read me many another stanza, all of which earned the same profuse praise and comment from him. There was nothing memorable about them; I could not even judge them to be much worse than the first one. Application, resignation, and chance had conspired in their composition; the virtues that Daneri attributed to them were afterthoughts. I realized that the poet's work had lain not in the poetry but in the invention of reasons for accounting the poetry admirable; naturally, that later work modified the poem for Daneri, but not for anyone else. His oral expression was extravagant; his metrical clumsiness prevented him, except on a very few occasions, from transmitting that extravagance to the poem.[1]

Only once in my lifetime have I had occasion to examine the fifteen thousand dodecasyllables of the *Polyalbion*—that topographical epic in which Michael Drayton recorded the fauna, flora, hydrography, orography, military and monastic history of England—but I am certain that Drayton's massive yet limited *oeuvre* is less tedious than the vast enterprise conceived and given birth by Carlos Argentino. He proposed to versify the entire planet; by 1941 he had already dispatched several hectares of the state of Queensland, more than a kilometer of the course of the Ob, a gasworks north of Veracruz, the leading commercial establishments in the parish of Concepción, Mariana Cambaceres de Alvear's villa on Calle Once de Setiembre in Belgrano, and a Turkish bath not far from the famed Brighton Aquarium. He read me certain laborious passages from the Australian region of his poem; his long, formless alexandrines lacked the relative agitation of the prologue. Here is one stanza:

> Hear this. To the right hand of the routine signpost
> (Coming—what need is there to say?—from north-northwest)
> Yawns a bored skeleton—Color? Sky-pearly.—
> Outside the sheepfold that suggests an ossuary.

"Two audacious risks!" he exclaimed in exultation, "snatched from the jaws of disaster, I can hear you mutter, by success! I admit it, I admit it. One, the epithet *routine*, while making an adjective of a synonym for 'highway,' nods, *en passant*, to the inevitable tedium inherent to those chores of a pastoral and rustic

1 I do, however, recall these lines from a satire in which he lashed out vehemently against bad poets:

> This one fits the poem with a coat of mail
> Of erudition; that one, with gala pomps and circumstance.
> Both flail their absurd pennons to no avail,
> Neglecting, poor wretches, the factor sublime—its LOVELINESS!

It was only out of concern that he might create an army of implacable and powerful enemies, he told me, that he did not fearlessly publish the poem.

nature that neither georgics nor our own belaureled *Don Segundo* ever dared acknowledge in such a forthright way, with no beating about the bush. And the second, delicately referring to the first, the forcefully prosaic phrase *Yawns a bored skeleton*, which the finicky will want to excommunicate without benefit of clergy but that the critic of more manly tastes will embrace as he does his very life. The entire line, in fact, is a good 24 karats. The second half-line sets up the most animated sort of conversation with the reader; it anticipates his lively curiosity, puts a question in his mouth, and then . . . *voilà*, answers it . . . on the instant. And what do you think of that coup *sky-pearly*? The picturesque neologism just *hints* at the sky, which is such an important feature of the Australian landscape. Without that allusion, the hues of the sketch would be altogether too gloomy, and the reader would be compelled to close the book, his soul deeply wounded by a black and incurable melancholy."

About midnight, I took my leave.

Two Sundays later, Daneri telephoned me for what I believe was the first time in his or my life. He suggested that we meet at four, "to imbibe the milk of the gods together in the nearby salon-bar that my estimable landlords, Messrs. Zunino and Zungri, have had the rare commercial foresight to open on the corner. It is a *café* you will do well to acquaint yourself with." I agreed, with more resignation than enthusiasm, to meet him. It was hard for us to find a table; the relentlessly modern "salon-bar" was only slightly less horrendous than I had expected; at neighboring tables, the excited clientele discussed the sums invested by Zunino and Zungri without a second's haggling. Carlos Argentino pretended to be amazed at some innovation in the establishment's lighting (an innovation he'd no doubt been apprised of beforehand) and then said to me somewhat severely:

"Much against your inclinations it must be that you recognize that this place is on a par with the most elevated heights of Flores."

Then he reread four or five pages of his poem to me. Verbal ostentation was the perverse principle that had guided his revisions: where he had formerly written "blue" he now had "azure," "cerulean," and even "bluish." The word "milky" was not sufficiently hideous for him; in his impetuous description of a place where wool was washed, he had replaced it with "lactine," "lactescent," "lactoreous," "lacteal." . . . He railed bitterly against his critics; then, in a more benign tone, he compared them to those persons "who possess neither precious metals nor even the steam presses, laminators, and sulfuric acids needed for minting treasures, but who can *point out* to others the *precise location* of a treasure." Then he was off on another tack, inveighing against the obsession for forewords, what he called "prologomania," an attitude that "had already been spoofed in the elegant preface to the *Quixote* by the Prince of Wits himself." He would, however, admit that an attention-getting recommendation might be a good idea at the portals of his new work—"an accolade penned by a writer of stature, of real import." He added that he was planning to publish the first cantos of his poem. It was at that point that I understood the unprecedented telephone call and the invitation: the man was about to ask me to write the preface to that pedantic farrago of his. But my fear turned out to be unfounded. Carlos Argentino remarked, with grudging admiration, that he believed he did not go too far in saying that the prestige achieved in every sphere by the man of letters Alvaro Melián Lafinur was "solid," and that if I could be persuaded to persuade him, Alvaro "might be enchanted to write the called-for foreword." In order to forestall the most unpardonable failure on my part, I was to speak on behalf of the poem's two incontrovertible virtues: its formal perfection and its scientific rigor—"because that broad garden of rhetorical devices, figures, charms, and graces will not tolerate a single detail that does not accord with its severe truthfulness." He added that Beatriz had always enjoyed Alvaro's company.

I agreed, I agreed most profusely. I did, however, for the sake of added plausibility, make it clear that I wouldn't be speaking with Alvaro on Monday but rather on Thursday, at the little supper that crowned each meeting of the Writers Circle. (There are no such suppers, although it is quite true that the meetings are held on Thursday, a fact that Carlos Argentino might verify in the newspapers and that lent a certain credence to my contention.) I told him (half-prophetically, half-farsightedly) that before broaching the subject of the prologue, I would describe the curious design of the poem. We said our good-byes; as I turned down Calle Bernardo de Irigoyen, I contemplated as impartially as I could the futures that were left to me: (a) speak with Alvaro and tell him that that first cousin of Beatriz' (the explanatory circumlocution would allow me to speak her name) had written a poem that seemed to draw out to infinity the possibilities of cacophony and chaos; (b) not speak with Alvaro. Knowing myself pretty well, I foresaw that my indolence would opt for (b).

From early Friday morning on, the telephone was a constant source of anxiety. I was indignant that this instrument from which Beatriz' irrecoverable voice had once emerged might now be reduced to transmitting the futile and perhaps angry complaints of that self-deluding Carlos Argentino Daneri. Fortunately, nothing came of it—save the inevitable irritation inspired by a man who had charged me with a delicate mission and then forgotten all about me.

Eventually the telephone lost its terrors, but in late October Carlos Argentino did call me. He was very upset; at first I didn't recognize his voice. Dejectedly and angrily he stammered out that that now unstoppable pair Zunino and Zungri, under the pretext of expanding their already enormous "*café*," were going to tear down his house.

"The home of my parents—the home where I was born—the old and deeply rooted house on Calle Garay!" he repeated, perhaps drowning his grief in the melodiousness of the phrase.

It was not difficult for me to share his grief. After forty, every change becomes a hateful symbol of time's passing; in addition, this was a house that I saw as alluding infinitely to Beatriz. I tried to make that extremely delicate point clear; my interlocutor cut me off. He said that if Zunino and Zungri persisted in their absurd plans, then Zunni, his attorney, would sue them *ipso facto* for damages, and force them to part with a good hundred thousand for his trouble.

Zunni's name impressed me; his law firm, on the corner of

Caseros and Tacuarí, is one of proverbial sobriety. I inquired whether Zunni had already taken the case. Daneri said he'd be speaking with him that afternoon; then he hesitated, and in that flat, impersonal voice we drop into when we wish to confide something very private, he said he had to have the house so he could finish the poem—because in one corner of the cellar there was an Aleph. He explained that an Aleph is one of the points in space that contain all points.

"It's right under the dining room, in the cellar," he explained. In his distress, his words fairly tumbled out. "*It's mine, it's mine;* I discovered it in my childhood, before I ever attended school. The cellar stairway is steep, and my aunt and uncle had forbidden me to go down it, but somebody said you could go around the world with that thing down there in the basement. The person, whoever it was, was referring, I later learned, to a steamer trunk, but I thought there was some magical contraption down there. I tried to sneak down the stairs, fell head over heels, and when I opened my eyes, I saw the Aleph."

"The Aleph?" I repeated.

"Yes, the place where, without admixture or confusion, all the places of the world, seen from every angle, coexist. I revealed my discovery to no one, but I did return. The child could not understand that he was given that privilege so that the man might carve out a poem! Zunino and Zungri shall never take it from me—never, *never!* Lawbook in hand, Zunni will prove that my Aleph is *inalienable.*"

I tried to think.

"But isn't the cellar quite dark?"

"Truth will not penetrate a recalcitrant understanding. If all the places of the world are within the Aleph, there too will be all stars, all lamps, all sources of light."

"I'll be right over. I want to see it."

I hung up before he could tell me not to come. Sometimes learning a fact is enough to make an entire series of corroborating details, previously unrecognized, fall into place; I was amazed that I hadn't realized until that moment that Carlos Argentino was a madman. All the Viterbos, in fact. . . .

Beatriz (I myself have said this many times) was a woman, a girl of implacable clearsightedness, but there were things about her—oversights, distractions, moments of contempt, downright cruelty—that perhaps could have done with a *pathological* explanation. Carlos Argentine's madness filled me with malign happiness; deep down, we had always detested one another.

On Calle Garay, the maid asked me to be so kind as to wait—Sr. Daneri was in the cellar, as he always was, developing photographs. Beside the flowerless vase atop the useless piano smiled the great faded photograph of Beatriz, not so much anachronistic as outside time. No one could see us; in a desperation of tenderness I approached the portrait.

"Beatriz, Beatriz Elena, Beatriz Elena Viterbo," I said. "Belovèd Beatriz, Beatriz lost forever—it's me, it's me, Borges."

Carlos came in shortly afterward. His words were laconic, his tone indifferent; I realized that he was unable to think of anything but the loss of the Aleph.

"A glass of pseudocognac," he said, "and we'll duck right into the cellar. I must forewarn you: dorsal decubitus is essential, as are darkness, immobility, and a certain ocular accommodation. You'll lie on the tile floor and fix your eyes on the nineteenth step of the pertinent stairway. I'll reascend the stairs, let down the trap door, and you'll be alone. Some rodent will frighten you—easy enough to do! Within a few minutes, you will see the Aleph. The microcosm of the alchemists and Kabbalists, our proverbial friend the *multum in parvo*, made flesh!

"Of course," he added, in the dining room, "if you don't see it, that doesn't invalidate anything I've told you. . . . Go on down; within a very short while you will be able to begin a dialogue with *all* the images of Beatriz."

I descended quickly, sick of his vapid chatter. The cellar, barely wider than the stairway, was more like a well or cistern. In vain my eyes sought the trunk that Carlos Argentino had mentioned. A few burlap bags and some crates full of bottles cluttered one corner. Carlos picked up one of the bags, folded it, and laid it out very precisely.

"The couch is a humble one," he explained, "but if I raise it one inch higher, you'll not see a thing, and you'll be cast down and dejected. Stretch that great clumsy body of yours out on the floor and count up nineteen steps."

I followed his ridiculous instructions; he finally left. He carefully let down the trap door; in spite of a chink of light that I began to make out later, the darkness seemed total. Suddenly I realized the danger I was in; I had allowed myself to be locked underground by a madman, after first drinking down a snifter of poison. Carlos' boasting clearly masked the deep-seated fear that I wouldn't see his "miracle"; in order to protect his delirium, in order to hide his madness from himself, *he had to kill me*. I felt a vague discomfort, which I tried to attribute to my rigidity, not to the operation of a narcotic. I closed my eyes, then opened them. It was then that I saw the Aleph.

I come now to the ineffable center of my tale; it is here that a writer's hopelessness begins. Every language is an alphabet of symbols the employment of which assumes a past shared by its interlocutors. How can one transmit to others the infinite Aleph, which my timorous memory can scarcely contain? In a similar situation, mystics have employed a wealth of emblems: to signify the deity, a Persian mystic speaks of a bird that somehow is all birds; Alain de Lille speaks of a sphere whose center is everywhere and circumference nowhere; Ezekiel, of an angel with four faces, facing east and west, north and south at once. (It is not for nothing that I call to mind these inconceivable analogies; they bear a relation to the Aleph.) Perhaps the gods would not deny me the discovery of an equivalent image, but then this report would be polluted with literature, with falseness. And besides, the central problem—the enumeration, even partial enumeration, of infinity—is irresolvable. In that unbounded moment, I saw millions of delightful and horrible acts; none amazed me so much as the fact that all occupied the same point, without superposition and without transparency. What my eyes saw was *simultaneous*; what I shall write is *successive*, because language is successive. Something of it, though, I will capture.

Under the step, toward the right, I saw a small iridescent sphere of almost unbearable brightness. At first I thought it was spinning; then I realized that the movement was an illusion produced by the dizzying spectacles inside it. The Aleph was probably two or three centimeters in diameter, but universal space was contained inside it, with no diminution in size. Each thing (the glass surface of a mirror, let us say) was infinite things, because I could clearly see it from every point in the cosmos. I saw the populous sea, saw dawn and dusk, saw the multitudes of the Americas, saw a silvery spiderweb at the center of a black pyramid, saw a broken labyrinth (it was London), saw endless eyes, all very close, studying themselves in me as though in a mirror, saw all the mirrors on the planet (and none of them reflecting me), saw in a rear courtyard on Calle Soler the same tiles I'd seen twenty years before in the entryway of a house in Fray Bentos, saw clusters of grapes, snow, tobacco, veins of metal, water vapor, saw convex equatorial deserts and their every grain of sand, saw a woman in Inverness whom I shall never forget, saw her violent hair, her haughty body, saw a cancer in her breast, saw a circle of dry soil within a sidewalk where there had once been a tree, saw a country house in Adrogué, saw a copy of the first English translation of Pliny (Philemon Holland's), saw every letter of every page at once (as a boy, I would be astounded that the letters in a closed book didn't get all scrambled up together overnight), saw simultaneous night and day, saw a sunset in Querétaro that seemed to reflect the color of a rose in Bengal, saw my bedroom (with no one in it), saw in a study in Alkmaar a globe of the terraqueous world placed between two mirrors that multiplied it endlessly, saw horses with wind-whipped manes on a beach in the Caspian Sea at dawn, saw the delicate bones of a hand, saw the survivors of a battle sending postcards, saw a Tarot card in a shopwindow in Mirzapur, saw the oblique shadows of ferns on the floor of a greenhouse, saw tigers, pistons, bisons, tides, and armies, saw all the ants on earth, saw a Persian astrolabe, saw in a desk drawer (and the handwriting made me tremble) obscene, incredible, detailed letters that Beatriz had sent Carlos Argentino, saw a beloved monument in Chacarita, saw the horrendous remains of what had once, deliciously, been Beatriz Viterbo, saw the circulation of my dark blood, saw the coils and springs of love and the alterations of death, saw the Aleph from everywhere at once, saw the earth in the Aleph, and the Aleph once more in the earth and the earth in the Aleph, saw my face and my viscera, saw your face, and I felt dizzy, and I wept, because my eyes had seen that secret, hypothetical object whose name has been usurped by men but which no man has ever truly looked upon: the inconceivable universe.

I had a sense of infinite veneration, infinite pity.

"Serves you right, having your mind boggled, for sticking your nose in where you weren't wanted," said a jovial, bored voice. "And you may rack your brains, but you'll never repay me for this revelation—not in a hundred years. What a magnificent observatory, eh, Borges!"

Carlos Argentino's shoes occupied the highest step. In the sudden half-light, I managed to get to my feet.

"Magnificent . . . Yes, quite . . . magnificent," I stammered.

The indifference in my voice surprised me.

"You did see it?" Carlos Argentino insisted anxiously. "See it clearly? In color and everything?"

Instantly, I conceived my revenge. In the most kindly sort of way—manifestly pitying, nervous, evasive—I thanked Carlos Argentino Daneri for the hospitality of his cellar and urged him to take advantage of the demolition of his house to remove himself from the pernicious influences of the metropolis, which no one—believe me, no one!—can be immune to. I refused, with gentle firmness, to discuss the Aleph; I clasped him by both shoulders as I took my leave and told him again that the country—peace and quiet, you know—was the very best medicine one could take.

Out in the street, on the steps of the Constitución Station, in the subway, all the faces seemed familiar. I feared there was nothing that had the power to surprise or astonish me anymore, I feared that I would never again be without a sense of *déjà vu*. Fortunately, after a few unsleeping nights, forgetfulness began to work in me again.

Postscript (March 1, 1943): Six months after the demolition of the building on Calle Garay, Procrustes Publishers, undaunted by the length of Carlos Argentino Daneri's substantial poem, published the first in its series of "Argentine pieces." It goes without saying what happened: Carlos Argentino won second place in the National Prize for Literature.[2] The first prize went to Dr. Aita; third, to Dr. Mario Bonfanti; incredibly, my own work *The Sharper's Cards* did not earn a single vote. Once more, incomprehension and envy triumphed! I have not managed to see Daneri for quite a long time; the newspapers say he'll soon be giving us another volume. His happy pen (belabored no longer by the Aleph) has been consecrated to setting the compendia of Dr. Acevedo Diaz to verse.

There are two observations that I wish to add: one, with regard to the nature of the Aleph; the other, with respect to its name. Let me begin with the latter: "aleph," as well all know, is the name of the first letter of the alphabet of the sacred language. Its application to the disk of my tale would not appear to be accidental. In the Kabbala, that letter signifies the En Soph, the pure and unlimited godhead; it has also been said that its shape is that of a man pointing to the sky and the earth, to indicate that the lower world is the map and mirror of the higher. For the *Mengenlehre*, the aleph is the symbol of the transfinite numbers, in which the whole is not greater than any of its parts. I would like to know: Did Carlos Argentino choose that name, or did he read it, *applied to another point at which all points converge*, in one of the innumerable texts revealed to him by the Aleph in his house? Incredible as it may seem, I believe that there is (or was) another Aleph; I believe that the Aleph of Calle Garay was a *false* Aleph.

Let me state my reasons. In 1867, Captain Burton was the British consul in Brazil; in July of 1942, Pedro Henríquez Ureña discovered a manuscript by Burton in a library in Santos, and in

2 "I received your mournful congratulations," he wrote me. "You scoff, my lamentable friend, in envy, but you shall confess—though the words stick in your throat!—that this time I have crowned my cap with the most scarlet of plumes; my turban, with the most caliphal of rubies."

this manuscript Burton discussed the mirror attributed in the East to Iskandar dhu-al-Qarnayn, or Alexander the Great of Macedonia. In this glass, Burton said, the entire universe was reflected. Burton mentions other similar artifices—the sevenfold goblet of Kai Khosru; the mirror that Ṭāriq ibn-Ziyād found in a tower (*1001 Nights*, 272); the mirror that Lucian of Samosata examined on the moon (*True History*, I:26); the specular spear attributed by the first book of Capella's *Satyricon* to Jupiter; Merlin's universal mirror, "round and hollow and . . . [that] seem'd a world of glas" (*Faerie Queene*, III:2,19)—and then adds these curious words: "But all the foregoing (besides sharing the defect of not existing) are mere optical instruments. The faithful who come to the Amr mosque in Cairo, know very well that the universe lies inside one of the stone columns that surround the central courtyard. . . . No one, of course, can see it, but those who put their ear to the surface claim to hear, within a short time, the bustling rumour of it. . . . The mosque dates to the seventh century; the columns were taken from other, pre-Islamic, temples, for as ibn-Khaldūn has written: *In the republics founded by nomads, the attendance of foreigners is essential for all those things that bear upon masonry.*"

Does that Aleph exist, within the heart of a stone? Did I see it when I saw all things, and then forget it? Our minds are permeable to forgetfulness; I myself am distorting and losing, through the tragic erosion of the years, the features of Beatriz.

For Estela Canto

[1945] [*AH*]

THE ZAHIR

In Buenos Aires the Zahir is a common twenty-centavo coin into which a razor or letter opener has scratched the letters *N T* and the number 2; the date stamped on the face is 1929. (In Gujarat, at the end of the eighteenth century, the Zahir was a tiger; in Java it was a blind man in the Surakarta mosque, stoned by the faithful; in Persia, an astrolabe that Nadir Shah ordered thrown into the sea; in the prisons of Mahdi, in 1892, a small sailors compass, wrapped in a shred of cloth from a turban, that Rudolf Karl von Slatin touched; in the synagogue in Córdoba, according to Zotenberg, a vein in the marble of one of the twelve hundred pillars; in the ghetto in Tetuán, the bottom of a well.) Today is the thirteenth of November; last June 7, at dawn, the Zahir came into my hands; I am not the man I was then, but I am still able to recall, and perhaps recount, what happened. I am still, albeit only partially, Borges.

On June 6, Teodelina Villar died. Back in 1930, photographs of her had littered the pages of worldly magazines; that ubiquity may have had something to do with the fact that she was thought to be a very pretty woman, although that supposition was not unconditionally supported by every image of her. But no matter—Teodelina Villar was less concerned with beauty than with perfection. The Jews and Chinese codified every human situation: the *Mishnah* tells us that beginning at sunset on the Sabbath, a tailor may not go into the street carrying a needle; the Book of Rites informs us that a guest receiving his first glass of wine must assume a grave demeanor; receiving the second, a respectful, happy air. The discipline that Teodelina Villar imposed upon herself was analogous, though even more painstaking and detailed. Like Talmudists and Confucians, she sought to make every action irreproachably correct, but her task was even more admirable and difficult than theirs, for the laws of her creed were not eternal, but sensitive to the whims of Paris and Hollywood. Teodelina Villar would make her entrances into orthodox places, at the orthodox hour, with orthodox adornments, and with orthodox world-weariness, but the world-weariness, the adornments, the hour, and the places would almost immediately pass out of fashion, and so come to serve (upon the lips of Teodelina Villar) for the very epitome of "tackiness." She sought the absolute, like Flaubert, but the absolute in the ephemeral. Her life was exemplary, and yet an inner desperation constantly gnawed at her. She passed through endless metamorphoses, as though fleeing from herself; her coiffure and the color of her hair were famously unstable, as were her smile, her skin, and the slant of her eyes. From 1932 on, she was studiedly thin. . . . The war gave her a great deal to think about. With Paris occupied by the Germans, how was one to follow fashion? A foreign man she had always had her doubts about was allowed to take advantage of her good will by selling her a number of stovepipe-shaped *chapeaux*. Within a year, it was revealed that those ridiculous shapes *had never been worn in Paris*, and therefore were not *hats*, but arbitrary and unauthorized *caprices*. And it never rains but it pours: Dr. Villar had to move to Calle Aráoz and his daughter's image began to grace advertisements for face creams and automobiles—face creams she never used and automobiles she could no longer afford! Teodelina knew that the proper exercise of her art required a great fortune; she opted to retreat rather than surrender. And besides—it pained her to compete with mere insubstantial *girls*. The sinister apartment on Aráoz, however, was too much to bear; on June 6, Teodelina Villar committed the breach of decorum of dying in the middle of Barrio Sur. Shall I confess that moved by the sincerest of Argentine passions—snobbery—I was in love with her, and that her death actually brought tears to my eyes? Perhaps the reader had already suspected that.

At wakes, the progress of corruption allows the dead person's body to recover its former faces. At some point on the confused night of June 6, Teodelina Villar magically became what she had been twenty years before; her features recovered the authority that arrogance, money, youth, the awareness of being the *crème de la crème*, restrictions, a lack of imagination, and stolidity can give. My thoughts were more or less these: No version of that face that had so disturbed me shall ever be as memorable as this one; really, since it could almost be the first, it ought to be the last. I left her lying stiff among the flowers, her contempt for the world growing every moment more perfect in death. It was about two o'clock, I would guess, when I stepped into the street. Outside, the predictable ranks of one- and two-story houses had taken on that abstract air they often have at night, when they are simplified by darkness and silence. Drunk with an almost impersonal pity, I wandered through the streets. On the corner of Chile and Tacuarí I spotted an open bar-and-general-store. In that establishment, to my misfortune, three men were playing *truco*.

In the rhetorical figure known as *oxymoron*, the adjective applied to a noun seems to contradict that noun. Thus, gnostics spoke of a "dark light" and alchemists, of a "black sun." Departing from my last visit to Teodelina Villar and drinking a glass of harsh brandy in a corner bar-and-grocery-store was a kind of oxymoron: the very vulgarity and facileness of it were what tempted me. (The fact that men were playing cards in the place increased the contrast. I asked the owner for a brandy and orange juice; among my change I was given the Zahir; I looked at it for an instant, then walked outside into the street, perhaps with the beginnings of a fever. The thought struck me that there is no coin that is not the symbol of all the coins that shine endlessly down throughout history and fable. I thought of Charon's obolus; the alms that Belisarius went about begging for; Judas' thirty pieces of silver; the drachmas of the courtesan Laïs; the ancient coin proffered by one of the Ephesian sleepers; the bright coins of the wizard in the *1001 Nights*, which turned into disks of paper; Isaac Laquedem's inexhaustible denarius; the sixty thousand coins, one for every line of an epic, which Firdusi returned to a king because they were silver and not gold; the gold doubloon nailed by Ahab to the mast; Leopold Bloom's unreturning florin; the gold louis that betrayed the fleeing Louis XVI near Varennes. As though in a dream, the thought that in any coin one may read those famous connotations seemed to me of vast, inexplicable importance. I wandered, with increasingly rapid steps, through the deserted streets and plazas. Weariness halted me at a corner. My eyes came to rest on a woebegone wrought-iron fence; behind it, I saw the black-and-white tiles of the porch of La Concepción. I had wandered in a circle; I was just one block from the corner where I'd been given the Zahir.

I turned the corner; the chamfered curb in darkness at the far end of the street showed me that the establishment had closed. On Belgrano I took a cab. Possessed, without a trace of sleepiness, almost happy, I reflected that there is nothing less material than money, since any coin (a twenty-centavo piece, for instance) is, in all truth, a panoply of possible futures. *Money is abstract*, I said over and over, *money is future time*. It can be an evening just outside the city, or a Brahms melody, or maps, or chess, or coffee, or the words of Epictetus, which teach contempt of gold; it is a Proteus more changeable than the Proteus of the isle of Pharos. It is unforeseeable time, Bergsonian time, not the hard, solid time of Islam or the Porch. Adherents of determinism deny that there is any event in the world that is *possible*, i.e., that *might* occur; a coin symbolizes our free will. (I had no suspicion at the time that these "thoughts" were an artifice against the Zahir and a first manifestation of its demonic influence.) After long and pertinacious musings, I at last fell asleep, but I dreamed that I was a pile of coins guarded by a gryphon.

The next day I decided I'd been drunk. I also decided to free myself of the coin that was affecting me so distressingly. I looked at it—there was nothing particularly distinctive about it, except those scratches. Burying it in the garden or hiding it in a corner of the library would have been the best thing to do, but I wanted to escape its orbit altogether, and so preferred to "lose" it. I went neither to the Basílica del Pilar that morning nor to the cemetery; I took a subway to Constitución and from Constitucíon to San Juan and Boedo. On an impulse, I got off at Urquiza; I walked toward the west and south; I turned left and right, with studied randomness, at several corners, and on a street that looked to me like all the others I went into the first tavern I came to, ordered a brandy, and paid with the Zahir. I half closed my eyes, even behind the dark lenses of my spectacles, and managed not to see the numbers on the houses or the name of the street. That night, I took a sleeping draft and slept soundly.

Until the end of June I distracted myself by composing a tale of fantasy. The tale contains two or three enigmatic circumlocutions—*sword-water* instead of *blood*, for example, and *dragon's-bed* for *gold*—and is written in the first person. The narrator is an ascetic who has renounced all commerce with mankind and lives on a kind of moor. (The name of the place is Gnitaheidr.) Because of the simplicity and innocence of his life, he is judged by some to be an angel; that is a charitable sort of exaggeration, because no one is free of sin—he himself (to take the example nearest at hand) has cut his father's throat, though it is true that his father was a famous wizard who had used his magic to usurp an infinite treasure to himself. Protecting this treasure from cankerous human greed is the mission to which the narrator has devoted his life; day and night he stands guard over it. Soon, perhaps too soon, that watchfulness will come to an end: the stars have told him that the sword that will sever it forever has already been forged. (The name of the sword is Gram.) In an increasingly tortured style, the narrator praises the lustrousness and flexibility of his body; one paragraph offhandedly mentions "scales"; another says that the treasure he watches over is of red rings and gleaming gold. At the end, we realize that the ascetic is the serpent Fafnir and the treasure on which the creature lies coiled is the gold of the Nibelungen. The appearance of Sigurd abruptly ends the story.

I have said that composing that piece of trivial nonsense (in the course of which I interpolated, with pseudoerudition, a line or two from the *Fafnismal*) enabled me to put the coin out of my mind. There were nights when I was so certain I'd be able to forget it that I would willfully remember it. The truth is, I abused those moments; starting to recall turned out to be much easier than stopping. It was futile to tell myself that that abominable nickel disk was no different from the infinite other identical, inoffensive disks that pass from hand to hand every day. Moved by that reflection, I attempted to think about another coin, but I couldn't. I also recall another (frustrated) experiment that I performed with Chilean five- and ten-centavo pieces and a Uruguayan two-centavo piece. On July 16, I acquired a pound sterling; I didn't look at it all that day, but that night (and others) I placed it under a magnifying glass and studied it in the light of a powerful electric lamp. Then I made a rubbing of it. The rays of light and the dragon and St. George availed me naught; I could not rid myself of my *idée fixe*.

In August, I decided to consult a psychiatrist. I did not confide the entire absurd story to him; I told him I was tormented by insomnia and that often I could not free my mind of the image of an object, any random object—a coin, say. . . . A short time later, in a bookshop on Calle Sarmiento, I exhumed a copy of Julius Barlach's *Urkunden zur Geschichte der Zahirsage* (Breslau, 1899).

Between the covers of that book was a description of my illness. The introduction said that the author proposed to "gather into a single manageable octavo volume every existing document that bears upon the superstition of the Zahir, including four articles held in the Habicht archives and the original manuscript of Philip Meadows Taylor's report on the subject." Belief in the Zahir is of Islamic ancestry, and dates, apparently, to sometime in the eighteenth century. (Barlach impugns the passages that Zotenberg attributes to Abul-Feddah.) In Arabic, "*zahir*" means visible, manifest, evident; in that sense, it is one of the ninety-nine names of God; in Muslim countries, the masses use the word for "beings or things which have the terrible power to be unforgettable, and whose image eventually drives people mad." Its first undisputed witness was the Persian polymath and dervish: Lutf Ali Azur; in the corroborative pages of the biographical encyclopedia titled *Temple of Fire*, Ali Azur relates that in a certain school in Shiraz there was a copper astrolabe "constructed in such a way that any man that looked upon it but once could think of nothing else, so that the king commanded that it be thrown into the deepest depths of the sea, in order that men might not forget the universe." Meadows Taylor's account is somewhat more extensive; the author served the Nazim of Hyderabad and composed the famous novel *Confessions of a Thug*. In 1832, on the outskirts of Bhuj, Taylor heard the following uncommon expression used to signify madness or saintliness: "Verily he has looked upon the tiger." He was told that the reference was to a magic tiger that was the perdition of all who saw it, even from a great distance, for never afterward could a person stop thinking about it. Someone mentioned that one of those stricken people had fled to Mysore, where he had painted the image of the tiger in a palace. Years later, Taylor visited the prisons of that district; in the jail at Nighur, the governor showed him a cell whose floor, walls, and vaulted ceiling were covered by a drawing (in barbaric colors that time, before obliterating, had refined) of an infinite tiger. It was a tiger composed of many tigers, in the most dizzying of ways; it was crisscrossed with tigers, striped with tigers, and contained seas and Himalayas and armies that resembled other tigers. The painter, a fakir, had died many years before, in that same cell; he had come from Sind or perhaps Gujarat and his initial purpose had been to draw a map of the world. Of that first purpose there remained some vestiges within the monstrous image. Taylor told this story to Muhammad al-Yemeni, of Fort William; al-Yemeni said that there was no creature in the world that did not tend toward becoming a *Zaheer*,[1] but that the All-Merciful does not allow two things to be a *Zaheer* at the same time, since a single one is capable of entrancing multitudes. He said that there is always a Zahir—in the Age of Ignorance it was the idol called Yahuk, and then a prophet from Khorasan who wore a veil spangled with precious stones or a mask of gold.[2] He also noted that Allah was inscrutable.

Over and over I read Barlach's monograph. I cannot sort out

1 This is Taylor's spelling of the word.

2 Barlach observes that Yahuk figures in the Qur'ān (71:23) and that the prophet is al-Moqanna (the Veiled Prophet) and that no one, with the exception of the surprising correspondent Philip Meadows Taylor, has ever linked those two figures to the Zahir.

my emotions; I recall my desperation when I realized that nothing could any longer save me, the inward relief of knowing that I was not to blame for my misfortune, the envy I felt for those whose Zahir was not a coin but a slab of marble or a tiger. How easy it is not to think of a tiger!, I recall thinking. I also recall the remarkable uneasiness I felt when I read this paragraph: "One commentator of the *Gulshan i Raz* states that 'he who has seen the Zahir soon shall see the Rose' and quotes a line of poetry interpolated into Aṭṭar's *Asrar Nama* ('The Book of Things Unknown'): 'the Zahir is the shadow of the Rose and the rending of the Veil.'"

On the night of Teodelina's wake, I had been surprised not to see among those present Sra. Abascal, her younger sister. In October, I ran into a friend of hers.

"Poor Julita," the woman said to me, "she's become so odd. She's been put into Bosch. How she must be crushed by those nurses spoon-feeding her! She's still going on and on about that coin, just like Morena Sackmann's chauffeur."

Time, which softens recollections, only makes the memory of the Zahir all the sharper. First I could see the face of it, then the reverse; now I can see both sides at once. It is not as though the Zahir were made of glass, since one side is not superimposed upon the other—rather, it is as though the vision were itself spherical, with the Zahir rampant in the center. Anything that is not the Zahir comes to me as though through a filter, and from a distance—Teodelina's disdainful image, physical pain. Tennyson said that if we could but understand a single flower we might know who we are and what the world is. Perhaps he was trying to say that there is nothing, however humble, that does not imply the history of the world and its infinite concatenation of causes and effects. Perhaps he was trying to say that the visible world can be seen entire in every image, just as Schopenhauer tells us that the Will expresses itself entire in every man and woman. The Kabbalists believed that man is a microcosm, a symbolic mirror of the universe; if one were to believe Tennyson, *everything* would be—*everything*, even the unbearable Zahir.

Before the year 1948, Julia's fate will have overtaken me. I will have to be fed and dressed, I will not know whether it's morning or night, I will not know who the man Borges was. Calling that future terrible is a fallacy, since none of the future's circumstances will in any way affect me. One might as well call "terrible" the pain of an anesthetized patient whose skull is being trepanned. I will no longer perceive the universe, I will perceive the Zahir. Idealist doctrine has it that the verbs "to live" and "to dream" are at every point synonymous; for me, thousands upon thousands of appearances will pass into one; a complex dream will pass into a simple one. Others will dream that I am mad, while I dream of the Zahir. When every man on earth thinks, day and night, of the Zahir, which will be dream and which reality, the earth or the Zahir?

In the waste and empty hours of the night I am still able to walk through the streets. Dawn often surprises me upon a bench in the Plaza Garay, thinking (or trying to think) about that passage in the *Asrar Nama* where it is said that the Zahir is the shadow of the Rose and the rending of the Veil. I link that pronouncement to this fact: In order to lose themselves in God, the Sufis repeat their own name or the ninety-nine names of God until the names mean nothing anymore. I long to travel that path. Perhaps by thinking about the Zahir unceasingly, I can manage to wear it away; perhaps behind the coin is God.

For Wally Zenner

[*1949*] [*AH*]

THE WRITING OF THE GOD

The cell is deep and made of stone; its shape is that of an almost perfect hemisphere, although the floor (which is also of stone) is something less than a great circle, and this fact somehow deepens the sense of oppression and vastness. A wall divides the cell down the center; though it is very high, it does not touch the top of the vault. I, Tzinacán, priest of the Pyramid of Qaholom, which Pedro de Alvarado burned, am on one side of the wall; on the other there is a jaguar, which with secret, unvarying paces measures the time and space of its captivity. At floor level, a long window with thick iron bars interrupts the wall. At the shadowless hour [midday] a small door opens above us, and a jailer (whom the years have gradually blurred) operates an iron pulley, lowering to us, at the end of a rope, jugs of water and hunks of meat. Light enters the vault; it is then that I am able to see the jaguar.

I have lost count of the years I have lain in this darkness; I who once was young and could walk about this prison do nothing now but wait, in the posture of my death, for the end the gods have destined for me. With the deep flint blade I have opened the breast of victims, but now I could not, without the aid of magic, lift my own body from the dust.

On the day before the burning of the Pyramid, the men who got down from their high horses scourged me with burning irons, to compel me to reveal the site of a buried treasure. Before my eyes they toppled the idol to the god, yet the god did not abandon me, and I held my silence through their tortures. They tore my flesh, they crushed me, they mutilated me, and then I awoke in this prison, which I will never leave alive.

Driven by the inevitability of doing *something*, of somehow filling time, I tried, in my darkness, to remember everything I knew. I squandered entire nights in remembering the order and the number of certain stone serpents, or the shape of a medicinal tree. Thus did I gradually conquer the years, thus did I gradually come to possess those things I no longer possessed. One night I sensed that a precise recollection was upon me; before the traveler sees the ocean, he feels a stirring in his blood. Hours later, I began to make out the memory; it was one of the legends of the god. On the first day of creation, foreseeing that at the end of time many disasters and calamities would befall, the god had written a magical phrase, capable of warding off those evils. He wrote it in such a way that it would pass down to the farthest generations, and remain untouched by fate. No one knows where he wrote it, or with what letters, but we do know that it endures, a secret text, and that one of the elect shall read it. I reflected that we were, as always, at the end of time, and that it would be my fate, as the last priest of the god, to be afforded the privilege of intuiting those words. The fact that I was bounded within a cell did not prevent me from harboring that hope; I might have seen Qaholom's inscription thousands of times, and need only to understand it.

That thought gave me spirit, and then filled me with a kind of vertigo. In the wide realm of the world there are ancient forms, incorruptible and eternal forms—any one of them might be the symbol that I sought. A mountain might be the word of the god, or a river or the empire or the arrangement of the stars. And yet, in the course of the centuries mountains are leveled and the path of a river is many times diverted, and empires know mutability and ruin, and the design of the stars is altered. In the firmament there is change. The mountain and the star are individuals, and the life of an individual runs out. I sought something more tenacious, more invulnerable. I thought of the generations of grain, of grasses, of birds, of men. Perhaps the spell was written upon my very face, perhaps I myself was the object of my search. Amid those keen imaginings was I when I recalled that one of the names of the god was jaguar—*tigre*.

At that, my soul was filled with holiness. I imagined to myself the first morning of time, imagined my god entrusting the message to the living flesh of the jaguars, who would love one another and engender one another endlessly, in caverns, in cane fields, on islands, so that the last men might receive it. I imagined to myself that web of tigers, that hot labyrinth of tigers, bringing terror to the plains and pastures in order to preserve the design. In the other cell, there was a jaguar; in its proximity I sensed a confirmation of my conjecture, and a secret blessing.

Long years I devoted to learning the order and arrangement of the spots on the tiger's skin. During the course of each blind day I was granted an instant of light, and thus was I able to fix in my mind the black shapes that mottled the yellow skin. Some made circles; others formed transverse stripes on the inside of its legs; others, ringlike, occurred over and over again—perhaps they were the same sound, or the same word. Many had red borders.

I will not tell of the difficulties of my labor. More than once I cried out to the vault above that it was impossible to decipher that text. Gradually, I came to be tormented less by the concrete enigma which occupied my mind than by the generic enigma of a message written by a god. What sort of sentence, I asked myself, would be constructed by an absolute mind? I reflected that even in the languages of humans there is no proposition that does not imply the entire universe; to say "the jaguar" is to say all the jaguars that engendered it, the deer and turtles it has devoured, the grass that fed the deer, the earth that was mother to the grass, the sky that gave light to the earth. I reflected that in the language of a god every word would speak that infinite concatenation of events, and not implicitly but explicitly, and not linearly but instantaneously. In time, the idea of a divine utterance came to strike me as puerile, or as blasphemous. A god, I reflected, must speak but a single word, and in that word there must be *absolute plenitude*. No word uttered by a god could be less than the universe, or briefer than the sum of time. The ambitions and poverty of human words—*all, world, universe*—are but shadows or simulacra of that Word which is the equivalent of a language and all that can be comprehended within a language.

One day or one night—between my days and nights, what difference can there be?—I dreamed that there was a grain of sand on the floor of my cell. Unconcerned, I went back to sleep; I dreamed that I woke up and there were two grains of sand. Again I slept; I dreamed that now there were three. Thus the grains of sand multiplied, little by little, until they filled the cell and I was dying beneath that hemisphere of sand. I realized that I was dreaming; with a vast effort I woke myself. But waking up was useless—I was suffocated by the countless sand. Someone said to me: *You have wakened not out of sleep, but into a prior dream, and that dream lies within another, and so on, to infinity, which is the number of the grains of sand. The path that you are to take is endless, and you will die before you have truly awakened.*

I felt lost. The sand crushed my mouth, but I cried out: *I cannot be killed by sand that I dream—nor is there any such thing as a dream within a dream.* A bright light woke me. In the darkness above me, there hovered a circle of light. I saw the face and hands of the jailer, the pulley, the rope, the meat, and the water jugs.

Little by little, a man comes to resemble the shape of his destiny; a man *is*, in the long run, his circumstances. More than a decipherer or an avenger, more than a priest of the god, I was a prisoner. Emerging from that indefatigable labyrinth of dreams, I returned to my hard prison as though I were a man returning home. I blessed its dampness, I blessed its tiger, I blessed its high opening and the light, I blessed my old and aching body, I blessed the darkness and the stone.

And at that, something occurred which I cannot forget and yet cannot communicate—there occurred union with the deity, union with the universe (I do not know whether there is a difference between those two words). Ecstasy does not use the same symbol twice; one man has seen God in a blinding light, another has perceived Him in a sword or in the circles of a rose. I saw a Wheel of enormous height, which was not before my eyes, or behind them, or to the sides, but everywhere at once.

This Wheel was made of water, but also of fire, and although I could see its boundaries, it was infinite. It was made of all things that shall be, that are, and that have been, all intertwined, and I was one of the strands within that all-encompassing fabric, and Pedro de Alvarado, who had tortured me, was another. In it were the causes and the effects, and the mere sight of that Wheel enabled me to understand all things, without end. O joy of understanding, greater than the joy of imagining, greater than the joy of feeling! I saw the universe and saw its secret designs. I saw the origins told by the Book of the People. I saw the mountains that rose from the water, saw the first men of wood, saw the water jars that turned against the men, saw the dogs that tore at their faces. I saw the faceless god who is behind the gods. I saw the infinite processes that shape a single happiness, and, understanding all, I also came to understand the writing on the tiger.

It is a formula of fourteen random (apparently random) words, and all I would have to do to become omnipotent is speak it aloud. Speaking it would make this stone prison disappear, allow the day to enter my night, make me young, make me immortal, make the jaguar destroy Alvarado, bury the sacred blade in Spanish breasts, rebuild the Pyramid, rebuild the empire. Forty syllables, fourteen words, and I, Tzinacán, would rule the lands once ruled by Moctezuma. But I know that I shall never speak those words, because I no longer remember Tzinacán.

Let the mystery writ upon the jaguars die with me. He who has glimpsed the universe, he who has glimpsed the burning designs of the universe, can have no thought for a man, for a man's trivial joys or calamities, though he himself be that man. He *was* that man, who no longer matters to him. What does he care about the fate of that other man, what does he care about the other man's nation, when now he is no one? That is why I do not speak the formula, that is why, lying in darkness, I allow the days to forget me.

For Ema Risso Platero

[*1949*] [*AH*]

THE SIMURGH AND THE EAGLE

Literarily speaking, what might be derived from the notion of a being composed of other beings, a bird, say, made up of birds?[1] Thus formulated, the problem appears to allow for merely trivial, if not actively unpleasant, solutions. One might suppose its possibilities to have been exhausted by the many-feathered, -eyed, -tongued, and -eared "*monstrum horrendum ingens*" [vast, horrible monster] that personifies Fame (or Scandal or Rumor) in Book IV of the *Aeneid*, or that strange king made of men who occupies the frontispiece of the *Leviathan*, armed with sword and staff. Francis Bacon (*Essays*, 1625) praised the first of these images; Chaucer and Shakespeare imitated it; no one, today, considers it any better than the "beast Acheron" who, according to the fifty-odd manuscripts of the *Visio Tundali*, stores sinners in the roundness of its belly, where they are tormented by dogs, bears, lions, wolves, and vipers.

In the abstract, the concept of a being composed of other beings does not appear promising: yet, in incredible fashion, one of the most memorable figures of Western literature, and another of Eastern literature, correspond to it. The purpose of this brief note is to describe these marvelous fictions, one conceived in Italy, the other in Nishapur.

The first is in Canto XVIII of the *Paradiso*. In his journey

1 Similarly, in Leibniz' *Monadology* (1714), we read that the universe consists of inferior universes, which in turn contain the universe, and so on *ad infinitum*.

through the concentric heavens, Dante observes a greater happiness in Beatrice's eyes and greater power in her beauty, and realizes that they have ascended from the ruddy heaven of Mars to the heaven of Jupiter. In the broader arc of this sphere, where the light is white, celestial creatures sing and fly, successively forming the letters of the phrase DILIGITE IUSTITIAM and the shape of an eagle's head, not copied from earthly eagles, of course, but directly manufactured by the Spirit. Then the whole of the eagle shines forth: it is composed of thousands of just kings. An unmistakable symbol of Empire, it speaks with a single voice, and says "I" rather than "we" (*Paradiso* XIX, 11). An ancient problem vexed Dante's conscience: Is it not unjust of God to damn, for lack of faith, a man of exemplary life who was born on the bank of the Indus and could know nothing of Jesus? The Eagle answers with the obscurity appropriate to a divine revelation: it censures such foolhardy questioning, repeats that faith in the Redeemer is indispensable, and suggests that God may have instilled this faith in certain virtuous pagans. It avers that among the blessed are the Emperor Trajan and Ripheus the Trojan, the former having lived just after and the latter before the Cross.[2] (Though resplendent in the fourteenth century, the Eagle's appearance is less effective in the twentieth, which generally reserves glowing eagles and tall, fiery letters for commercial propaganda. Cf. Chesterton, *What I Saw in America*, 1922.)

That anyone has ever been able to surpass one of the great figures of the *Commedia* seems incredible, and rightly so: nevertheless, the feat has occurred. A century after Dante imagined the emblem of the Eagle, Farid al-Din Attar, a Persian of the Sufi sect, conceived of the strange Simurgh (Thirty Birds), which implicitly encompasses and improves upon it. Farid al-

2 Pompeo Venturi disapproves of the election of Ripheus, a personage who until this apotheosis had existed only in a few lines of the *Aeneid* (II, 339, 426). Virgil declares him the most just of the Trojans and adds to the report of his end the resigned ellipsis: "*Dies aliter visum*" [The gods ruled otherwise]. There is not another trace of him in all of literature. Perhaps Dante chose him as a symbol by virtue of his vagueness. Cf. the commentaries of Casini (1921) and Guido Vitali (1943).

Din Attar was born in Nishapur,[3] land of turquoises and swords. In Persian, Attar means "he who traffics in drugs." In the *Lives of the Poets*, we read that such indeed was his trade. One afternoon, a dervish entered the apothecary's shop, looked over its many jars and pillboxes, and began to weep. Attar, astonished and disturbed, begged him to leave. The dervish answered: "It costs me nothing to go, since I carry nothing with me. As for you, it will cost you greatly to say good-bye to the treasures I see here." Attar's heart went as cold as camphor. The dervish left, but the next morning, Attar abandoned his shop and the labors of this world.

A pilgrim to Mecca, he crossed Egypt, Syria, Turkestan, and the north of India; on his return, he gave himself over to literary composition and the fervent contemplation of God. It is a fact of some renown that he left behind twenty thousand distichs: his works are entitled *The Book of the Nightingale, The Book of Adversity, The Book of Instruction, The Book of Mysteries, The Book of Divine Knowledge, The Lives of the Saints, The King and the Rose, A Declaration of Wonders*, and the extraordinary *Conference of the Birds (Mantiq al-Tayr)*. In the last years of his life, which is said to have reached a span of one hundred and ten years, he renounced all worldly pleasures, including those of versification. He was put to death by the soldiers of Tule, son of Genghis Khan. The vast image I have alluded to is the basis of the *Mantiq al-Tayr*, the plot of which is as follows:

The faraway king of all the birds, the Simurgh, lets fall a magnificent feather in the center of China: tired of their age-old anarchy, the birds resolve to go in search of him. They know that their king's name means thirty birds; they know his palace is located on the Kaf, the circular mountain that surrounds the earth.

They embark upon the nearly infinite adventure. They pass through seven valleys or seas; the name of the penultimate is Vertigo; the last, Annihilation. Many pilgrims give up; others perish. Thirty, purified by their efforts, set foot on the mountain

3 Katibi, author of the *Confluence of the Two Seas*, declared: "I am of the garden of Nishapur, like Attar, but I am the thorn of Nishapur and he was the rose."

of the Simurgh. At last they gaze upon it: they perceive that they are the Simurgh and that the Simurgh is each one of them and all of them. In the Simurgh are the thirty birds and in each bird is the Simurgh.[4] (Plotinus, too—*The Enneads* V, 8.4—asserts a paradisiacal extension of the principle of identity: "Everywhere in the intelligible heaven is all, and all is all and each all. The sun, there, is all the stars; and every star, again, is all the stars and sun.")

The disparity between the Eagle and the Simurgh is no less obvious than their resemblance. The Eagle is merely implausible; the Simurgh, impossible. The individuals who make up the Eagle are not lost in it (David serves as the pupil of one eye; Trajan, Ezekiel, and Constantine as brows); the birds that gaze upon the Simurgh are at the same time the Simurgh. The Eagle is a transitory symbol, as were the letters before it; those who form its shape with their bodies do not cease to be who they are: the ubiquitous Simurgh is inextricable. Behind the Eagle is the personal God of Israel and Rome; behind the magical Simurgh is pantheism.

A final observation. The imaginative power of the legend of the Simurgh is apparent to all; less pronounced, but no less real, is its rigor and economy. The pilgrims go forth in search of an unknown goal; this goal, which will be revealed only at the end, must arouse wonder and not be or appear to be merely added on. The author finds his way out of this difficulty with classical elegance; adroitly, the searchers are what they seek. In identical fashion, David is the secret protagonist of the story told him by Nathan (II Samuel 12); in identical fashion, De Quincey has proposed that the individual man Oedipus, and not man in general, is the profound solution to the riddle of the Theban Sphinx.

[1948] *[EA]*

4 Silvina Ocampo (*Espacios métricos*, 12) has put this episode into verse:

Era Dios ese pájaro como un enorme espejo:
los contenía a todos; no era un mero reflejo.
En sus plumas hallaron cada uno sus plumas
en los ojos, los ojos con memorias de plumas.

[Like an enormous mirror this bird was God:/containing them all, and not a mere reflection./In his feathers each one found his own feathers/in his eyes, their eyes with memories of feathers.]

A NEW REFUTATION OF TIME

Vor mir keine Zeit, nach mir wird keine seyn.
Mit mir gebiert sie sich, mit mir geht sie auch ein.
[Before me there was no time, after me there will be none./With me it is born, with me it will also die.]

—DANIEL VON CZEPKO, SEXCENTA MONIDISTICHA SAPIENTUM III, II (1655)

PRELIMINARY NOTE

Had this refutation (or its title) been published in the middle of the eighteenth century, it would be included in a bibliography by Hume, or at least mentioned by Huxley or Kemp Smith. But published in 1947 (after Bergson) it is the anachronistic *reductio ad absurdum* of an obsolete system, or even worse, the feeble artifice of an Argentine adrift on a sea of metaphysics. Both conjectures are plausible and perhaps even true, but I cannot promise some startling new conclusion on the basis of my rudimentary dialectics. The thesis I shall expound is as old as Zeno's arrow or the chariot of the Greek king in the *Milinda Pañha*; its novelty, if any, consists in applying to my ends the classic instrument of Berkeley. Both he and his successor David Hume abound in paragraphs that contradict or exclude my thesis; nonetheless, I believe I have deduced the inevitable consequence of their doctrine.

The first article (A) was written in 1944 and appeared in number 115 of *Sur*; the second, from 1946, is a revision of the first. I have deliberately refrained from making the two into one, deciding that two similar texts could enhance the reader's comprehension of such an unwieldy subject.

A word on the title: I am not unaware that it is an example of that monster called a *contradictio in adjecto* by logicians, for to say that a refutation of time is new (or old, for that matter) is to recognize a temporal predicate that restores the very notion the subject intends to destroy. But I shall let this fleeting joke stand to prove, at least, that I do not exaggerate the importance of wordplay. In any case, language is so saturated and animated by time that, quite possibly, not a single line in all these pages fails to require or invoke it.

I dedicate these exercises to my ancestor Juan Crisótomo Lafinur (1797–1824), who left a memorable poem or two to Argentine letters and who strove to reform the teaching of philosophy by refining out traces of theology and by explaining the theories of Locke and Condillac in his courses. He died in exile: as with all men, it was his lot to live in bad times.[1]

Buenos Aires, December 23, 1946

A

I

In the course of a life dedicated to belles-lettres and, occasionally, to the perplexities of metaphysics, I have glimpsed or foreseen a refutation of time, one in which I myself do not believe, but which tends to visit me at night and in the hours of weary twi-

1 All expositions of Buddhism mention the *Milinda Pañha*, an Apology from the second century; this work recounts a debate between the king of the Bactrians, Menander, and the monk Nagasena. The latter argues that just as the king's chariot is not the wheels nor the chassis nor the axle nor the shaft nor the yoke, neither is man matter nor form nor impressions nor ideas nor instincts nor consciousness. He is not the combination of those parts, nor does he exist outside them. . . . After this discussion, which lasts several days, Menander (Milinda) converts to the faith of the Buddha. The *Milinda Pañha* has been rendered into English by Rhys Davids (Oxford, 1890–94).

light with the illusory force of a truism. This refutation is to be found, in one form or another, in all of my books. It is prefigured in the poems "Inscription on Any Tomb" and "Truco" in my *Fervor of Buenos Aires* (1923); it is openly stated on a certain page of *Evaristo Carriego*; and in the story "Feeling in Death," which I transcribe below. None of these texts satisfies me, not even the last on the list, which is less logical and explanatory than sentimental and divinatory. I will attempt, in this present writing, to establish a basis for them all.

Two arguments led me to this refutation of time: Berkeley's idealism and Leibniz's principle of indiscernibles.

Berkeley (*The Principles of Human Knowledge, par. 3*) observed:

> That neither our thoughts, nor passions, nor ideas formed by the imagination, exist without the mind is what everybody will allow. And to me it is no less evident that the various *Sensations* or *ideas imprinted on the sense,* however blended or combined together (that is, whatever *objects* they compose), cannot exist otherwise than in a mind perceiving them. . . . The table I write on, I say exists, that is, I see and feel it; and if I were out of my study I should say it existed—meaning thereby that if I was in my study I might perceive it, or that some other spirit actually does perceive it. . . . For as to what is said of the absolute existence of unthinking things without any relation to their being perceived, that is to me perfectly unintelligible. Their *esse* is *percipi*, nor is it possible they should have any existence out of the minds or thinking things which perceive them.

In paragraph 23 he added, foreseeing objections:

> But, say you, surely there is nothing easier than for me to imagine trees, for instance, in a park, or books existing in a closet, and nobody by to perceive them. I answer, you may so, there is no difficulty in it; but what is all this, I beseech you, more than framing in *your* mind certain ideas which you call books and trees, and at the same time omitting to frame the idea of anyone that may perceive them? But do not you yourself perceive or

> think of them all the while? This therefore is nothing to the purpose; it only shews you have the power of imagining or forming ideas in your mind: but it doth not shew that you can conceive it possible that the objects of your thought may exist without the mind.

In another paragraph, number 6, he had already declared:

> Some truths there are so near and obvious to the mind that a man need only open his eyes to see them. Such I take this important one to be, viz., that all the choir of heaven and furniture of the earth, in a word all those bodies which compose the mighty frame of the world have not any subsistence without a mind—that their *being* is *to be perceived or known;* that consequently so long as they are not actually perceived by me, or do not exist in my mind or that of any other created spirit, they must either have no existence at all, or else subsist in the mind of some Eternal Spirit.

Such is, in the words of its inventor, the idealist doctrine. To understand it is easy; the difficulty lies in thinking within its limitations. Schopenhauer himself, in expounding it, is guilty of some negligence. In the first lines of his book *Die Welt als Wille und Vorstellung*—from the year 1819—he formulates the following declaration, which makes him a creditor as regards the sum total of imperishable human perplexity: "The world is my representation. The man who confesses this truth clearly understands that he does not know a sun nor an earth, but only some eyes which see a sun and a hand which feels an earth." That is, for the idealist Schopenhauer, a man's eyes and hands are less illusory or unreal than the earth or the sun. In 1844 he publishes a supplementary volume. In the first chapter he rediscovers and aggravates the previous error: he defines the universe as a cerebral phenomenon, and he distinguishes between the "world in the head" and the "world outside the head." Berkeley, nevertheless, will have made his Philonous say, in 1713: "The brain therefore you speak of, being a sensible thing, exists only in the mind. Now, I would fain know whether you think it reasonable to suppose, that one idea or thing existing in the mind, occasions all other ideas. And if you think so, pray how do you account for the origin of that primary idea or brain itself?" To Schopenhauer's dualism, or cerebralism, Spiller's monism may legitimately be counterposed. Spiller (*The Mind of Man* [1902], chap. 8) argues that the retina, and the cutaneous surface invoked to explain visual and tactile phenomena, are in turn two tactile and visual systems, and that the room we see (the "objective" one) is no greater than the imagined ("cerebral") one, and that the former does not contain the latter, since two independent visual systems are involved. Berkeley (*The Principles of Human Knowledge*, 10 and 116) likewise denied primary qualities—the solidity and extension of things—or the existence of absolute space.

Berkeley affirmed the continuous existence of objects, inasmuch as when no individual perceives them, God does. Hume, with greater logic, denied this existence (*A Treatise of Human Nature* I, 4, 2). Berkeley affirmed personal identity, "for I myself am not my ideas, but somewhat else, a thinking, active principle that perceives" (*Dialogues*, 3). Hume, the skeptic, refuted this belief, and made each man "a bundle or collection of different perceptions, which succeed each other with an inconceivable rapidity" (I, 4, 6). Both men affirmed the existence of time: for Berkeley it is "the succession of ideas in my mind, flowing uniformly, and participated in by all beings" (*The Principles of Human Knowledge*, 98). For Hume, it is "a succession of indivisible moments" (I, 2, 2).

I have accumulated quotations from the apologists of idealism, I have provided their canonical passages, I have reiterated and explained, I have censured Schopenhauer (not without ingratitude), to help my reader penetrate this unstable world of the mind. A world of evanescent impressions; a world without matter or spirit, neither objective nor subjective; a world without the ideal architecture of space; a world made of time, of the absolute uniform time of the *Principia;* an inexhaustible labyrinth, a chaos, a dream—the almost complete disintegration that David Hume reached.

Once the idealist argument is accepted, I believe that it is possible—perhaps inevitable—to go further. For Hume, it is not justifiable to speak of the form of the moon or its color: its form and color are the moon. Neither can one speak of the mind's perceptions, inasmuch as the mind is nothing but a series of perceptions. The Cartesian "I think, therefore I am" is thus invalid: to say I think is to postulate the I, a *petitio principii.* In the eighteenth century, Lichtenberg proposed that instead of "I think," we should say impersonally "It thinks," as we say "It thunders" or "There is lightning." I repeat: there is not, behind the face, a secret self governing our acts or receiving our impressions; we are only the series of those imaginary acts and those errant impressions. The series? If we deny matter and spirit, which are continuities, and if we also deny space, I do not know what right we have to the continuity that is time. Let us imagine a present moment, any one at all. A night on the Mississippi. Huckleberry Finn wakes up. The raft, lost in the shadows of twilight, continues downstream. It may be a bit cold. Huckleberry Finn recognizes the soft, ceaseless sound of the water. Negligently he opens his eyes: he sees an indefinite number of stars, a nebulous line of trees. Then he sinks into a sleep without memories, as into dark waters.[2] Metaphysical idealism declares that to add to these perceptions a material substance (the object) and a spiritual substance (the subject) is precarious and vain. I maintain that it is no less illogical to think that they are terms in a series whose beginning is as inconceivable as its end. To add to the river and the riverbank perceived by Huck the notion of yet another substantive river with another riverbank, to add yet another perception to that immediate network of perceptions, is altogether unjustifiable in the eyes of idealism. In my eyes, it is no less unjustifiable to add a chronological precision: for instance, the fact that the abovementioned event should have taken place on the night of June 7, 1849, between 4:10 and 4:11. In other words, I deny, using the arguments of idealism, the vast temporal series that idealism

2 For the reader's convenience I have chosen a moment between two intervals of sleep, a literary, not a historical, instant. If anyone suspects a fallacy, he can insert another example, if he wants, one from his own life.

permits. Hume denied the existence of an absolute space, in which each thing has its place; I deny the existence of one single time, in which all events are linked. To deny coexistence is no less difficult than to deny succession.

I deny, in a large number of instances, the existence of succession. I deny, in a large number of instances, simultaneity as well. The lover who thinks, "While I was so happy, thinking about the faithfulness of my beloved, she was busy deceiving me," is deceiving himself. If every state in which we live is absolute, that happiness was not concurrent with that betrayal. The discovery of that betrayal is merely one more state, incapable of modifying "previous" states, though not incapable of modifying their recollection. Today's misfortune is no more real than yesterday's good fortune. I will look for a more concrete example: At the beginning of August 1824, Captain Isidoro Suárez, at the head of a squadron of Peruvian hussars, assured the Victory of Junín; at the beginning of August 1824, De Quincey issued a diatribe against *Wilhelm Meisters Lehrjahre;* these deeds were not contemporaneous (they are now), inasmuch as the two men died—the one in the city of Montevideo, the other in Edinburgh—knowing nothing of each other. . . . Every instant is autonomous. Not vengeance nor pardon nor jails nor even oblivion can modify the invulnerable past. No less vain to my mind are hope and fear, for they always refer to future events, that is, to events which will not happen to us, who are the diminutive present. They tell me that the present, the "specious present" of the psychologists, lasts between several seconds and the smallest fraction of a second, which is also how long the history of the universe lasts. Or better, there is no such thing as "the life of a man," nor even "one night in his life." Each moment we live exists, not the imaginary combination of these moments. The universe, the sum total of all events, is no less ideal than the sum of all the horses—one, many, none?—Shakespeare dreamed between 1592 and 1594. I might add that if time is a mental process, how can it be shared by countless, or even two different men?

The argument set forth in the preceding paragraphs, interrupted and encumbered by examples, may seem intricate. I shall try a more direct method. Let us consider a life in which repetitions abound: my life, for instance. I never pass the Recoleta cemetery without remembering that my father, my grandparents, and my great-grandparents are buried there, as I shall be; then I remember that I have remembered the same thing many times before; I cannot stroll around the outskirts of my neighborhood in the solitude of night without thinking that night is pleasing to us because, like memory, it erases idle details; I cannot lament the loss of a love or a friendship without reflecting how one loses only what one really never had; each time I cross one of the southside corners, I think of you, Helena; each time the air brings me the scent of eucalyptus I think of Adrogué in my childhood; each time I recall fragment 91 of Heraclitus, "You cannot step into the same river twice," I admire his dialectical skill, for the facility with which we accept the first meaning ("The river is another") covertly imposes upon us the second meaning ("I am another") and gives us the illusion of having invented it; each time I hear a Germanophile deride Yiddish, I reflect that Yiddish is, after all, a German dialect, barely tainted by the language of the Holy Ghost. These tautologies (and others I shall not disclose) are my whole life. Naturally, they recur without design; there are variations of emphasis, temperature, light, general physiological state. I suspect, nonetheless, that the number of circumstantial variants is not infinite: we can postulate, in the mind of an individual (or of two individuals who do not know each other but in whom the same process is operative), two identical moments. Once this identity is postulated, we may ask: Are not these identical moments the same moment? Is not one single repeated terminal point enough to disrupt and confound the series in time? Are the enthusiasts who devote themselves to a line of Shakespeare not literally Shakespeare?

I am still not certain of the ethics of the system I have outlined, nor do I know whether it exists. The fifth paragraph of chapter IV in the *Sanhedrin* of the Mishnah declares that, in the eyes of God, he who kills a single man destroys the world. If there is no plurality, he who annihilated all men would be no more guilty than the primitive and solitary Cain—an orthodox view—nor more global in his destruction—which may be magic, or so I understand it. Tumultuous and universal catastrophes—fires, wars, epidemics—are but a single sorrow, multiplied in many illusory mirrors. Thus Bernard Shaw surmises (*Guide to Socialism*, 86):

> What you yourself can suffer is the utmost that can be suffered on earth. If you starve to death, you experience all the starvation that ever has been or ever can be. If ten thousand other women starve to death with you, their suffering is not increased by a single pang: their share in your fate does not make you ten thousand times as hungry, nor prolong your suffering ten thousand times. Therefore do not be oppressed by "the frightful sum of human suffering": there is no sum. . . . Poverty and pain are not cumulative.

(Cf. also C. S. Lewis, *The Problem of Pain* VII.)

Lucretius (*De rerum natura* I, 830) attributes to Anaxagoras the doctrine that gold consists of particles of gold; fire, of sparks; bone, of imperceptible little bones. Josiah Royce, perhaps influenced by St. Augustine, proposes that time is made up of time and that "every now within which something happens is therefore *also* a succession" (*The World and the Individual* II, 139). That proposition is compatible with my essay.

II

All language is of a successive nature; it does not lend itself to reasoning on eternal, intemporal matters. Those readers who are displeased with the preceding arguments may prefer this note from 1928, titled "Feeling in Death," which I mentioned earlier:

> I wish to record here an experience I had some nights ago, a trifling matter too evanescent and ecstatic to be called an adventure, too irrational and sentimental to be called a thought. I am speaking of a scene and its word, a word I had said before but had not lived with total involvement until that night. I shall de-

scribe it now, with the incidents of time and place that happened to reveal it. This is how I remember it: I had spent the afternoon in Barracas, a place I rarely visited, a place whose distance from the scene of my later wanderings lent a strange aura to that day. As I had nothing to do that night and the weather was fair, I went out after dinner to walk and remember. I had no wish to have a set destination; I followed a random course, as much as possible; I accepted, with no conscious anticipation other than avoiding the avenues or wide streets, the most obscure invitations of chance. A kind of familiar gravitation, however, drew me toward places whose name I shall always remember, for they arouse in me a certain reverence. I am not speaking of the specific surroundings of my childhood, my own neighborhood, but of its still mysterious borders, which I have possessed in words but little in reality, a zone that is familiar and mythological at the same time. The opposite of the known—its reverse side—are those streets to me, almost as completely hidden as the buried foundation of our house or our invisible skeleton. My walk brought me to a corner. I breathed the night, in peaceful respite from thought. The vision before me, in no way complicated, in any case seemed simplified by my fatigue. It was so typical that it seemed unreal. It was a street of low houses, and although the first impression was poverty, the second was undoubtedly joyous. The street was both very poor and very lovely. No house stood out on the street; a fig tree cast a shadow over a corner wall; the street doors—higher than the lines extending along the walls—seemed made of the same infinite substance as the night. The sidewalk sloped up the street, a street of elemental clay, the clay of a still unconquered America. Farther away, the narrow street dwindled into the pampa, toward Maldonado. Over the muddy, chaotic earth a red pink wall seemed not to harbor moonglow but to shed a light of its own. There is probably no better way to name tenderness than that red pink.

I stood looking at that simple scene. I thought, no doubt aloud: "This is the same as it was thirty years ago. . . ." I guessed at the date: a recent time in other countries, but already remote in this changing part of the world. Perhaps a bird was singing and I felt for him a small, bird-size affection; but most probably the only noise in this vertiginous silence was the equally timeless sound of the crickets. The easy thought *I am somewhere in the 1800s* ceased to be a few careless words and became profoundly real. I felt dead, I felt I was an abstract perceiver of the world, struck by an undefined fear imbued with science, or the supreme clarity of metaphysics. No, I did not believe I had traversed the presumed waters of Time; rather I suspected that I possessed the reticent or absent meaning of the inconceivable word *eternity*. Only later was I able to define these imaginings.

Now I shall transcribe it thus: that pure representation of homogeneous facts—calm night, limpid wall, rural scent of honeysuckle, elemental clay—is not merely identical to the scene on that corner so many years ago; it is, without similarities or repetitions, the same. If we can intuit that sameness, time is a delusion: the impartiality and inseparability of one moment of time's apparent yesterday and another of time's apparent today are enough to make it disintegrate.

It is evident that the number of these human moments is not infinite. The basic elemental moments are even more impersonal—physical suffering and physical pleasure, the approach of sleep, listening to a single piece of music, moments of great intensity or great dejection. I have reached, in advance, the following conclusion: life is too impoverished not to be also immortal. But we do not even possess the certainty of our poverty, inasmuch as time, easily denied by the senses, is not so easily denied by the intellect, from whose essence the concept of succession seems inseparable. So then, let my glimpse of an idea remain as an emotional anecdote; let the real moment of ecstasy and the possible insinuation of eternity which that night lavished on me, remain confined to this sheet of paper, openly unresolved.

B

Of the many doctrines recorded in the history of philosophy, idealism is perhaps the most ancient and most widely divulged. The observation is Carlyle's (*Novalis*, 1829). Without hope of completing the infinite list, one could add to the philosophers he mentioned the Platonists, for whom the only realities are archetypes (Norris, Judah Abrabanel, Gemistus, Plotinus); the theologians, for whom everything that is not the divinity is provisional (Malebranche, Johannes Eckhart); the monists, who make the universe a vain adjective of the Absolute (Bradley, Hegel, Parmenides). . . . Idealism is as ancient as metaphysical angst. Its most clever apologist, George Berkeley, flourished in the eighteenth century. Contrary to what Schopenhauer declared (*Die Welt als Wille und Vorstellung* II, 1), his merit did not consist in the intuitive perception of that doctrine, but in the arguments he conceived to rationalize it. Berkeley used those arguments against the notion of matter; Hume applied them to consciousness; I propose to apply them to time. First I shall briefly summarize the various stages of this dialectic.

Berkeley denied matter. This did not mean, of course, that he denied colors, smells, tastes, sounds, and tactile sensations; what he denied was that aside from these perceptions—components of the external world—there might be something invisible, intangible, called matter. He denied that there were pains no one feels, colors no one sees, forms no one touches. He argued that to add matter to perceptions is to add to the world another inconceivable and superfluous world. He believed in the world of appearances fabricated by our senses, but he considered that the material world (Toland's, say) was an illusory duplication. He observed (*The Principles of Human Knowledge*, para. 3):

> That neither our thoughts, nor passions, nor ideas formed by the imagination, exist without the mind, is what everybody will allow. And to me it is no less evident that the various *sensations* or *ideas imprinted on the sense*, however blended or combined together (that is, whatever *objects* they compose), cannot exist otherwise than in a mind perceiving them. . . . The table I write on I say exists, that is, I see and feel it; and if I were out of my study I should say it existed—meaning thereby that if I was in my study I might perceive it, or that some other spirit actually does perceive it. . . . For as to what is said of the absolute existence of unthinking things without any relation to their being perceived, that is to me perfectly unintelligible. Their *esse* is *per-*

> *cipi*, nor is it possible they should have any existence out of the minds or thinking things which perceive them.

Foreseeing objections, he added in paragraph 23:

> But, say you, surely there is nothing easier than for me to imagine trees, for instance, in a park, or books existing in a closet, and nobody by to perceive them. I answer, you may so, there is no difficulty in it; but what is all this, I beseech you, more than framing in *your* mind certain ideas which you call books and trees, and at the same time omitting to frame the idea of any one that may perceive them? But do not you yourself perceive or think of them all the while? This therefore is nothing to the purpose; it only shews you have the power of imagining or forming ideas in your mind: but it does not shew that you can conceive it possible the objects of your thought may exist without the mind.

In paragraph 6 he had already stated:

> Some truths there are so near and obvious to the mind that a man need only open his eyes to see them. Such I take this important one to be, viz., that all the choir of heaven and furniture of the earth, in a word all those bodies which compose the mighty frame of the world, have not any subsistence without a mind—that their *being* is *to be perceived or known*; that consequently so long as they are not actually perceived by me, or do not exist in my mind or that of any other created spirit, they must either have no existence at all, or else subsist in the mind of some Eternal Spirit.

(Berkeley's God is a ubiquitous spectator whose purpose is to give coherence to the world.)

The doctrine I have just explained has been perversely interpreted. Herbert Spencer believed he had refuted it (*The Principles of Psychology* VIII, 6), arguing that if nothing exists outside consciousness, then consciousness must be infinite in time and space. The first is evident if we understand that all time is time perceived by someone, but erroneous if we infer that this time must necessarily embrace an infinite number of centuries; the second is illicit, inasmuch as Berkeley repeatedly denied an absolute space (*The Principles of Human Knowledge*, 116; *Siris*, 266). Even more indecipherable is the error Schopenhauer made (*Die Welt als Wille und Vorstellung* II, 1) when he held that for the idealists the world is a cerebral phenomenon. Berkeley, however, had written (*Dialogues between Hylas and Philonous* II): "The brain . . . being a sensible thing, exists only in the mind. Now, I would fain know whether you think it reasonable to suppose, that one idea or thing existing in the mind, occasions all other ideas. And if you think so, pray how do you account for the origin of that primary idea or brain itself?" The brain, in truth, is no less a part of the external world than the constellation Centaurus.

Berkeley denied that there was an object behind sense impressions. David Hume denied that there was a subject behind the perception of changes. Berkeley denied matter; Hume denied the spirit. Berkeley did not wish us to add the metaphysical notion of matter to the succession of impressions; Hume did not wish us to add the metaphysical notion of a self to the succession of mental states. This expansion of Berkeley's arguments is so logical that Berkeley had already foreseen it (as Alexander Campbell Fraser noted), and had even tried to dispute it by means of the Cartesian *ergo sum*. Hylas, foreshadowing Hume, had said in the third and last of the *Dialogues*: "In consequence of your own principles, it should follow that you are only a system of floating ideas, without any substance to support them. Words are not to be used without a meaning. And as there is no more meaning in spiritual substance than in material substance, the one is to be exploded as well as the other." Hume corroborates this (*A Treatise of Human Nature* I, 4, 6):

> [We] are nothing but a bundle or collection of different perceptions, which succeed each other with an inconceivable rapidity. . . . The mind is a kind of theater, where several perceptions successively make their appearance; pass, repass, glide away, and mingle in an infinite variety of postures and situations. . . .

> The comparison of the theater must not mislead us. They are the successive perceptions only, that constitute the mind; nor have we the most distant notion of the place, where these scenes are represented, or of the materials of which it is composed.

Having admitted the idealist argument, I believe it is possible—perhaps inevitable—to go further. For Berkeley, time is "the succession of ideas in my mind, which flows uniformly and is participated in by all beings" (*The Principles of Human Knowledge*, 98); for Hume, it is "a succession of indivisible moments" (*A Treatise of Human Nature* I, 2, 3). However, with the continuities of matter and spirit denied, with space denied, I do not know by what right we retain that continuity which is time. Outside each perception (real or conjectural), matter does not exist; outside each mental state, spirit does not exist; neither then must time exist outside each present moment. Let us choose a moment of the utmost simplicity, for example, Chuang Tzu's dream (Herbert Allen Giles, *Chuang Tzu*, 1899). Some twenty-four centuries ago, Chuang Tzu dreamed he was a butterfly, and when he awoke he was not sure whether he was a man who had dreamed he was a butterfly or a butterfly who dreamed he was a man. Let us not consider the awakening, but the moment of the dream itself, or one of its moments. "I dreamed I was a butterfly fluttering through the air knowing nothing at all of Chuang Tzu," says the ancient text. We shall never know whether Chuang Tzu saw a garden over which he seemed to fly, or a moving yellow triangle, which was doubtlessly himself, but it is clear that the image was subjective, even though it was supplied to him by memory. The doctrine of psychophysical parallelism will avow that this image must have resulted from a change in the dreamer's nervous system; according to Berkeley, at that moment the body of Chuang Tzu did not exist, nor did the dark bedroom in which he was dreaming, save as a perception in the mind of God. Hume simplifies what happened even more: at that moment the spirit of Chuang Tzu did not exist; all that existed were the colors of the dream and the certainty of his being a butterfly. He existed as a momentary term in the "bundle or collection of different perceptions" which constituted, some four centuries before Christ, the mind of Chuang Tzu; he existed as the term n in an infinite temporal series, between $n - 1$ and $n + 1$. There is no other reality for idealism than mental processes; to add an objective butterfly to the butterfly one perceives therefore seems a vain duplication; to add a self to the mental processes seems, therefore, no less exorbitant. Idealism holds that there was a dreaming, a perceiving, but not a dreamer nor even a dream; it holds that to speak of objects and subjects is to fall into an impure mythology. Now then, if each psychic state is self-sufficient, if to connect it to a circumstance or an ego is an illicit and idle addition, with what right do we later assign it a place in time? Chuang Tzu dreamed he was a butterfly, and during the course of that dream he was not Chuang Tzu but a butterfly. With space and self abolished, how can we link those dreaming moments to his waking moments and the feudal age of Chinese history? This does not mean that we shall never know, even if only approximately, the date of that dream; I merely mean that the chronological determination of an event, of any event in the world, is alien and exterior to the event. In China, the dream of Chuang Tzu is proverbial; let us imagine that one of its almost infinite readers dreams he is a butterfly and then that he is Chuang Tzu. Let us imagine that, by a not impossible chance, this dream repeats exactly the dream of the master. Having postulated such an identity, we may well ask: Are not those coinciding moments identical? Is not *one single repeated term* enough to disrupt and confound the history of the world, to reveal that there is no such history?

To deny time involves two negations: denying the succession of the terms in a series, and denying the synchronism of terms in two series. In fact, if each term is absolute, its relations are reduced to the consciousness that those relations exist. One state precedes another if it knows it is anterior; state G is contemporaneous with state H if it knows it is contemporaneous. Contrary to Schopenhauer's statement in his table of fundamental truths (*Die Welt als Wille und Vorstellung* II, 4), each fraction of time does not fill all space simultaneously:

time is not ubiquitous.[3] (Of course, at this stage in the argument, space no longer exists.)

Meinong, in his theory of apprehension, admits the apprehension of imaginary objects: the fourth dimension, say, or Condillac's sentient statue, or Lotze's hypothetical animal, or the square root of minus one. If the reasons I have indicated are valid, then matter, the ego, the external world, universal history, our lives, also belong to that nebulous sphere.

Furthermore, the phrase "negation of time" is ambiguous. It can mean the eternity of Plato or Boethius and also the dilemmas of Sextus Empiricus. The latter (*Adversus mathematicos* XI, 197) denies the past, which already was, and the future, which is not yet, and argues that the present is either divisible or indivisible. It is not indivisible, for in that case it would have no beginning to connect it to the past nor end to connect it to the future, nor even a middle, because whatever has no beginning or end has no middle. Neither is it divisible, for in that case it would consist of a part that was and another that is not. *Ergo*, the present does not exist, and since the past and the future do not exist either, time does not exist. F. H. Bradley rediscovers and improves upon this conundrum: he observes (*Appearance and Reality* IV) that if the now can be divided into other nows, it is no less complicated than time; and that if it is indivisible, time is merely a relation between intemporal things. Such reasoning, obviously, denies the parts in order to deny the whole; I reject the whole in order to exalt each one of the parts. Via the dialectic of Berkeley and Hume, I have arrived at Schopenhauer's dictum:

> The form of the appearance of the will is only the present, not the past or the future; the latter do not exist except in the concept and by the linking of the consciousness, so far as it follows the principle of reason. No man has ever lived in the past, and none will live in the future; the present alone is the form of all

3 Newton had previously asserted: "Each particle of space is eternal, each indivisible moment of duration is everywhere" (*Principia* III, 42).

> life, and is a possession that no misfortune can take away. . . . We might compare time to an infinitely revolving circle: the half that is always sinking would be the past, that which is always rising would be the future; but the indivisible point at the top which the tangent touches, would be the present. Motionless like the tangent, that extensionless present marks the point of contact of the object, whose form is time, with the subject, which has no form because it does not belong to the knowable but is the precondition of all knowledge. (*Die Welt als Wille und Vorstellung* I, 54)

A fifth-century Buddhist treatise, the *Visuddhimagga*, or *The Path to Purity*, illustrates the same doctrine with the same figure: "Strictly speaking, the life of a being lasts as long as an idea. Just as a rolling carriage wheel touches earth at only one point, so life lasts as long as a single idea" (Radhakrishnan, *Indian Philosophy* I, 373). Other Buddhist texts say that the world is annihilated and resurges six billion five hundred million times a day and that every man is an illusion, vertiginously wrought by a series of solitary and momentary men. "The man of a past moment," *The Path to Purity* advises us, "has lived, but he does not live nor will he live; the man of a future moment will live, but he has not lived nor does he now live; the man of the present moment lives, but he has not lived nor will he live" (I, 407), a dictum we may compare with Plutarch's "Yesterday's man died in the man of today, today's man dies in the man of tomorrow" (*De E apud Delphos*, 18).

And yet, and yet . . . To deny temporal succession, to deny the self, to deny the astronomical universe, appear to be acts of desperation and are secret consolations. Our destiny (unlike the hell of Swedenborg and the hell of Tibetan mythology) is not terrifying because it is unreal; it is terrifying because it is irreversible and iron-bound. Time is the substance of which I am made. Time is a river that sweeps me along, but I am the river; it is a tiger that mangles me, but I am the tiger; it is a fire that consumes me, but I am the fire. The world, unfortunately, is real; I, unfortunately, am Borges.

Freund, es ist auch genug. Im Fall du mehr willst lesen,
So geh und werde selbst die Schrift und selbst das Wesen.
[Friend, this is enough. Should you wish to read more,/Go and yourself become the writing, yourself the essence.]

—ANGELUS SILESIUS, CHERUBINISCHER WANDERSMANN VI, 263 (1675)

[1944–46] *[SJL]*

PARADISO XXXI, 108

Diodorus Siculus tells the story of a god who had been cut into pieces and then scattered; which of us, strolling at dusk or recollecting a day from the past, has never felt that something of infinite importance has been lost?

Mankind has lost a face, an irretrievable face. At one time everyone wanted to be the pilgrim who was dreamed up in the Empyrean under the sign of the Rose, the one who sees the Veronica in Rome and fervently mutters: "Christ Jesus, my God, truly God: so this is what your face was like?"

There is a stone face by a road and an inscription that reads: "Authentic Portrait of the Holy Face of the Christ of Jaén." If we really knew what that face had been like, we would possess the key to the parables and we would know whether the son of the carpenter was also the Son of God.

Paul saw it as a light that knocked him to the ground. John saw it as the sun shining with all its strength. Teresa of Ávila often saw it bathed in a serene light, but she could never quite make out the color of the eyes.

These features have been lost to us the way a kaleidoscope design is lost forever, or a magic number composed of everyday figures. We can be looking at them and still not know them. The profile of a Jewish man in the subway may well be the same as Christ's; the hands that make change for us at the ticket window could be identical to the hands that soldiers one day nailed to the cross.

Some feature of the crucified face may lurk in every mirror. Maybe the face died and faded away so that God could be everyman.

Who knows? We might see it tonight in the labyrinths of sleep and remember nothing in the morning.

[*1960*] [*KK*]

EPILOGUE
to *Dreamtigers*

God willing, the underlying monotony of this collection will be less apparent than the geographic and historical diversity of its themes. Time has brought these pieces together, not I: it has approved old works I haven't had the courage to revise, because I wrote them with a different idea of literature in mind. Of all the books I have delivered to the printer, none, I think, is as personal as this unruly jumble, this florilegium, for the simple reason that it is rich in reflections and interpolations. Little has happened in my life, but I have read a great deal, which is to say I have found few things more memorable than Schopenhauer's ideas and the verbal music of England.

A man sets himself the task of portraying the world. Over the years he fills a given surface with images of provinces and kingdoms, mountains, bays, ships, islands, fish, rooms, instruments, heavenly bodies, horses, and people. Shortly before he dies he discovers that this patient labyrinth of lines is a drawing of his own face.

—J.L.B.
Buenos Aires, October 31, 1960

[*1960*] [*KK*]

POEM OF THE GIFTS

No one should read self-pity or reproach
into this statement of the majesty
of God, who with such splendid irony
granted me books and blindness at one touch.

Care of this city of books he handed over
to sightless eyes, which now can do no more
than read in libraries of dream the poor
and senseless paragraphs that dawns deliver

to wishful scrutiny. In vain the day
squanders on these same eyes its infinite tomes,
as distant as the inaccessible volumes
that perished once in Alexandria.

From hunger and from thirst (in the Greek story),
a king lies dying among gardens and fountains.
Aimlessly, endlessly, I trace the confines,
high and profound, of this blind library.

Cultures of East and West, the entire atlas,
encyclopedias, centuries, dynasties,
symbols, the cosmos, and cosmogonies
are offered from the walls, all to no purpose.

In shadow, with a tentative stick, I try
the hollow twilight, slow and imprecise—

I, who had always thought of Paradise
in form and image as a library.

Something, which certainly is not defined
by the word *fate*, arranges all these things;
another man was given, on other evenings
now gone, these many books. He too was blind.

Wandering through the gradual galleries,
I often feel with vague and holy dread
I am that other dead one, who attempted
the same uncertain steps on similar days.

Which of the two is setting down this poem—
a single sightless self, a plural I?
What can it matter, then, the name that names me,
given our curse is common and the same?

Groussac[1] or Borges, now I look upon
this dear world losing shape, fading away
into a pale uncertain ashy-gray
that feels like sleep, or else oblivion.

[*1960*] [*AR*]

1 Paul Groussac (1845–1929), Argentine critic and man of letters, and a predecessor of Borges as director of the National Library, also suffered from the accompanying irony of blindness.

MATTHEW XXV: 30

The first bridge, Constitution Station. At my feet
the shunting trains trace iron labyrinths.
Steam hisses up and up into the night,
which becomes at a stroke the night of the Last Judgment.

From the unseen horizon
and from the very center of my being,
an infinite voice pronounced these things—
things, not words. This is my feeble translation,
time-bound, of what was a single limitless Word:

"Stars, bread, libraries of East and West,
playing-cards, chessboards, galleries, skylights, cellars,
a human body to walk with on the earth,
fingernails, growing at nighttime and in death,
shadows for forgetting, mirrors busily multiplying,
cascades in music, gentlest of all time's shapes.
Borders of Brazil, Uruguay, horses and mornings,
a bronze weight, a copy of the Grettir Saga,
algebra and fire, the charge at Junín in your blood,
days more crowded than Balzac, scent of the honeysuckle,
love and the imminence of love and intolerable remembering,
dreams like buried treasure, generous luck,
and memory itself, where a glance can make men dizzy—
all this was given to you, and with it
the ancient nourishment of heroes—
treachery, defeat, humiliation.

In vain have oceans been squandered on you, in vain
the sun, wonderfully seen through Whitman's eyes.
You have used up the years and they have used up you,
and still, and still, you have not written the poem."

[*1964*] [*AR*]

ON SALVATION BY DEEDS

One autumn, one of the autumns of time, the Shinto divinities gathered, not for the first time, at Izumo. They are said to have numbered eight million. Being a shy man I would have felt a bit lost among so many. In any case, it is not convenient to deal in inconceivable numbers. Let us say there were eight, since eight is a good omen in these islands.

They were downcast, but did not show it: the visages of divinities are undecipherable kanji. They seated themselves in a circle on the green crest of a hill. They had been observing mankind from their firmament or from a stone or from a snowflake. One of the divinities spoke:

Many days, or centuries, ago, we gathered here to create Japan and the world. The fishes, the seas, the seven colors of the rainbow, the generations of plants and animals have all worked out well. So that men should not be burdened with too many things, we gave them succession, issue, the plural day and the singular night. We also bestowed on them the gift of experimenting with certain variations. The bee continues repeating beehives. But man has imagined devices: the plow, the key, the kaleidoscope. He also imagined the sword and the art of war. He has just imagined an invisible weapon which could put an end to history. Before this senseless deed is done, let us wipe out men.

They remained pensive. Without haste another divinity spoke:

It's true. They have thought up that atrocity, but there is also this something quite different, which fits in the space encompassed by seventeen syllables.

The divinity intoned them. They were in an unknown language, and I could not understand them.

The leading divinity delivered a judgment:

Let men survive.

Thus, because of a *haiku*, the human race was saved.

IZUMO, APRIL 27, 1984

[*1984*] [*AK*]

PATIO

With evening
the two or three colors of the patio grew weary.
Tonight, the moon's bright circle
does not dominate outer space.
Patio, heaven's watercourse.
The patio is the slope
down which the sky flows into the house.
Serenely
eternity waits at the crossway of the stars.
It is lovely to live in the dark friendliness
of covered entrance way, arbor, and wellhead.

[1923] [*RF*]

II.

THROUGH THE LOOKING GLASS

GEORGE SANTAYANA

The poet and philosopher Santayana (this enumeration obeys the order of his activities) was born toward the end of 1863 in Madrid. In 1872, his parents took him to America. They were Catholics. Santayana deplores his lost faith, "that splendid error so harmonious with the impulses and ambitions of the soul." As one North American writer put it: "Santayana believes there is no God and that the Holy Virgin is the mother of God."

He received his Ph.D. at Harvard in 1886. Eight years later he published his first book: *Sonnets and Poems*. Then, in 1906, the five volumes of his famous *Life of Reason: Reason in Common Sense, Reason in Society, Reason in Religion, Reason in Art, Reason in Science*. Now he repudiates those volumes; not their doctrine, but their method.

Although won over by the music of English, Santayana—a Spaniard, after all—is a materialist. "I'm a committed materialist, perhaps the only one. I don't pretend to know what matter is; let the physicists explain it; whatever it is, I resolutely call it matter, just as I call my acquaintances Smith or Jones, without knowing their secrets." And then: "Dualism is the awkward conjunction of a robot and a phantom." Regarding idealism, it might or might not be the source of truth, but because the world has been behaving for thousands of years as if our perceptions were correct, the wisest path would be to go along with such a pragmatic endorsement and trust in the future.

Christianity (he says elsewhere) is a poor literal translation of Jewish metaphors.

Now, after many years of teaching metaphysics at Harvard University, he lives in England. England (he says) is the home par excellence of honest happiness and of the tranquil pleasure of being oneself.[1]

[*1937*] [*SJL*]

1 Santayana's works are numerous and include: *Three Philosophical Poets* (1910), *Winds of Doctrine* (1913), *Soliloquies in England* (1922), *Skepticism and Animal Faith* (1923), *Dialogues in Limbo* (1925), *Platonism and the Spiritual Life* (1927), *The Realm of Being* (1928), and *The Realm of Matter* (1930).

THOMAS MANN ON SCHOPENHAUER

Glory tends to malign great men, and no one more vehemently, perhaps, than Schopenhauer. The face of a decrepit monkey and an ill-humored anthology (under the lurid title of *Love, Women and Death*, the auspicious preference of some ne'er-do-well publisher) represent him in the eyes of Spain and of these Americas. Philosophy professors tolerate or encourage this error. There are those who reduce him to pessimism, a reduction as innocuous and laughable as that of ranking Leibniz an optimist. Mann, on the other hand, reasons that Schopenhauer's pessimism is an inseparable facet of his doctrine: "All the manuals," he observes, "explain that Schopenhauer was, first of all, a philosopher of the Will and, secondly, of pessimism. But there is neither a first nor second: Schopenhauer, a philosopher and psychologist of the Will, could not not be a pessimist. The Will is something fundamentally unhappy, that is, anxiety, needs, greed, appetite, longing, pain. The world of the will must be, by definition, a world of suffering . . ." I think that optimism and pessimism are qualitative or subjective judgments which have nothing to do with Schopenhauer's vocation, that is, metaphysics.

He was also a consummate writer. Other philosophers such as Berkeley, Hume, Henri Bergson, and William James say exactly what they set out to say but lack the passion, the persuasive virtues of Schopenhauer. The well-known influence he exercised over Wagner and Nietzsche is undeniable.

Thomas Mann in his book on Schopenhauer (1938) notes that Schopenhauer's philosophy befits a young man. He cites

Nietzsche's opinion that every philosophy reflects the age of its thinker and that Schopenhauer's cosmic poem bears the mark of a youthful age ruled by Eros and a sense of death.

In his elegant summary, the author of *The Magic Mountain* does not mention another book, which is Schopenhauer's principal work, *The World as Will and Representation.* I suspect that if he had reread it, he would have also mentioned that slightly horrifying and phantasmagorical *Parerga and Paralipomena*, in which Schopenhauer reduces all persons in the universe to incarnations or masks of a single being (who is, predictably, the Will) and declares that all the events in our lives, as unfortunate as they may be, are mere inventions of our ego—like the disasters in a dream.

[*1939*] [*SJL*]

BERKELEY'S CROSSROADS

In a previous essay titled "The Nothingness of Personality," I have laid out many ramifications of the same line of reasoning that this new essay is intended to explain.[1] That tortuous text, excessively literary, is merely a series of suggestions and examples, arrayed one after another yet with no argumentative continuity. In order to remedy this defect, I have decided, in the following lines, to expound upon the hypothesis that I felt so moved to discuss in the first place. Thus, situating the reader alongside me, at the very wellspring of my thoughts, touching together upon the difficulties as they arise while slipping lively and free-flowing thoughts through the same conduit, we shall set off hand in hand on this eternal adventure that is metaphysics.

My incentive was Berkeley's subjective idealism. To assuage those readers in whose memories the aforementioned theory does not loom in massive relief, be it because it has been too long since some professor displayed his indifference to it, or—an even more forgivable distraction—because it had never been frequented in the first place, it is worth summarizing briefly the main points of that doctrine.

Esse rerum est percipi: to be is to be perceived:[2] things do

1 This essay was written in 1923, one year after "La nadería de la personalidad": "frivolity" or "inconsequentiality" would actually be closer to the connotation of "nadería" which has been translated in a literal manner as "nothingness." [SJL]

2 Borges incorrectly cites Berkeley's original Latin phrase, *Esse es percipi*, adding "rerum" or the genitive "of things" which prefigures his use of Berkeley's original idea in his 1940 story "Tlön, Uqbar, Orbis Tertius." [SJL]

not exist until they have been observed. The illustrious structure of Berkeley's system is based upon and yet elevates this inspired dictum, this spare formula with which he dispels the artful fiction of dualism and unveils for us the fact that reality is not a distant riddle, intractable and difficult to decipher, but rather an intimate nearness, easily reached and open on all sides. Let us examine the details of his argument.

We'll choose any concrete idea, for example, what the words *fig tree* denote. Clearly, the concept as named is nothing but an abbreviation for many different perceptions: to our eyes, the fig tree is a lowly, twisted trunk above which extends a bright abundance of leaves; to our hands, it is the rounded toughness of the wood and the roughness of the leaves; to our palates, only the covetable flavor of the fruit exists. There are, furthermore, olfactory and auditory perceptions that I will purposefully leave aside to avoid overly complicating the matter, though they cannot really be ignored.

All of these, according to the nonmetaphysical man, are different characteristics of the tree. But if we delve deeper into this simple assertion, we'll be alarmed by the many confusions and contradictions that it conceals.

And so, while anyone would admit that greenness is not an essential quality of a fig tree, since at nightfall its brightness wanes, its leaves turn yellow, and its trunk becomes dark and blackened, everyone agrees in the assertion that convexity and bulk are inherent realities of the tree. As far as taste is concerned, the issue becomes a bit convoluted. No one supposes that the flavor of a fruit has no need for our palate in order to exist in its maximum fullness. From distinction to distinction, we may approach the dualism nowadays defended by physics, a questionable arrangement that, according to the well-conceived definition articulated by the British Hegelian Francis Bradley, involves considering some qualities of reality as nouns and others as adjectives.

By general rule, substance is assigned only size, while all other characteristics—color, taste, and sound—are considered beholden to a borderland between the spiritual and the material, an intermediate universe or the outskirts that are forged, in a continual and secret collaboration, between spatial reality and our organs of perception. This conjecture suffers from grave flaws. The pure and simple naked expanse that, according to the dualists and materialists, composes the essence of the world is a useless trifle: blind, vain, formless, without bulk, neither soft nor hard, an abstraction that no one manages to visualize. The act of assigning it substance is a desperate measure of the antimetaphysical prejudice that completely fails to deny the essential reality of the external world and that takes refuge in a shady compromise by tossing it a verbal bit of charity: a hypocrisy comparable to the concept of atoms, imagined only as a defense against the idea of infinite divisibility.

Berkeley, in a decisive line of reasoning, gets to the root of the problem:

> That neither our Thoughts, nor Passions, nor Ideas formed by the Imagination, exist without the Mind, is what every Body will allow. And it seems no less evident that the various Sensations or Ideas imprinted on the Sense, however blended or combined together (that is, whatever Objects they compose) cannot exist otherwise than in a Mind perceiving them . . .
>
> The Table I write on, I say, exists, that is, I see and feel it; and if I were out of my Study I should say it existed, meaning thereby that if I was in my Study I might perceive it, or that some other Spirit actually does perceive it. There was an Odor, that is, it was smelled; There was a Sound, that is to say, it was heard; a Colour or Figure, and it was perceived by Sight or Touch. This is all that I can understand by these and the like Expressions. For as to what is said of the absolute Existence of unthinking Things without any relation to their being perceived, that seems perfectly unintelligible. Their Esse is Percipi, nor is it possible they should have any Existence, out of the Minds or thinking Things which perceive them.[3]

3 George Berkeley, *A Treatise Concerning the Principles of Human Knowledge* (1734), Part I, paragraph 3.

In another place he writes, to head off objections:

> But say you, surely there is nothing easier than to imagine Trees, for instance, in a Park, or Books existing in a Closet, and no Body by to perceive them. I answer, you may so, there is no difficulty in it: But what is all this, I beseech you, more than framing in your Mind certain Ideas which you call Books and Trees, and the same time omitting to frame the Idea of any one that may perceive them? But do not you your self perceive or think of them all the while?[4]

And, expanding his argument:

> Some Truths there are so near and obvious to the Mind, that a Man need only open his Eyes to see them. Such I take this Important one to be, to wit, that all the Choir of Heaven and Furniture of the Earth, in a word all those Bodies which compose the mighty Frame of the World, have not any Subsistence without a Mind, that their Being is to be perceived or known; that consequently so long as they are not actually perceived by me, or do not exist in my Mind or that of any other created Spirit, they must either have no Existence at all, or else subsist in the Mind of some eternal Spirit.[5]

Berkeley the Philosopher wrote the above lines, save for the final line in which Berkeley the Bishop appears. The distinction is very important since if Berkeley, in the capacity of a thinking man, could pick apart the universe according to his whim, such freedom was unspeakable in his role as serious prelate, versed in theology and implacable in the certainty of his ability to see the entirety of truth. God served as the mortar with which he connected the disparate pieces of the universe or, more accurately, he was the nexus for the scattered accountings of different perceptions and ideas. Berkeley affirmed this, stating that the complex totality of life is nothing other than a procession

4 Ibid. Part I, paragraph 23.

5 Ibid. Part I, paragraph 6.

of ideas in God's consciousness and that whatever our senses perceive is but a faint glimmer of the universal vision that unfolds from his spirit. According to this concept, God is not the maker of things; rather, he is life's meditator, or an immortal and ubiquitous spectator of living. His eternal vigilance prevents the universe from being annihilated and resurrected by capricious individual ministrations, and lends solidity and weighty prestige to the entire system. (Berkeley forgets that, once cognition and being are made equal, things such as autonomous existence cease to be and thus only metaphorically could be said to annihilate and resurrect.)

Moving away from such solemn sophisms, more fit to be spoken than understood, I wish to show, by submitting the spirit to the exact argument that he applies to matter, where the fundamental fallacy in Berkeley's doctrine is hiding.

Berkeley asserts: Things only exist once they have been observed by the mind. It is fair to respond: Yes, but the mind only exists as a perceiver and meditator of things. Thus, not only the unity of the external world but also that of the spiritual world is broken down. The object deteriorates, together with the subject. Both enormous nouns, spirit and matter, evaporate at once and life returns to being a tangled mass of states of mind, a dream with no dreamer. There's no reason to suffer from the confusion wrought by this doctrine, since it concerns only the imaginary collective of every moment of life, leaving the order and accuracy of each one of them, and even small, partial groupings of them, in peace. What does turn to smoke are the great metaphysical continuities: the I, space, time . . . Indeed, if external attention determines the existence of things, if these things cannot exist except from within a mind that thinks of or is aware of them, what are we to make, for example, of the succession of pleasant, impartial and painful feelings which, linked together, make up my life? Where is my past? Think of the feebleness of memory and you'll accept without reservation that it is not contained within me. I am limited to this vertiginous present and it is inadmissible that the dreadful thousands of loose moments could fit within its abject narrowness. If you prefer not to appeal to miracles by invoking, in favor of your beleaguered zeal for unity, the help of an omnipotent God who embraces and passes through everything as light moves through a crystal, you'll agree with me about the utter triviality of those grandiose words: *I, Space, Time* . . .

In defense of the first, the famous bastion of *cogito, ergo sum* will do you no good. I think, therefore I am. If that Latin meant *I think, therefore thinking exists*—the only conclusion that logically follows from the premise—the truth of it would be as incontrovertible as it is useless. Employed to mean *I think, therefore a thinker exists*, is precise in the sense that all action supposes a subject, and fallacious in terms of the ideas of individuation and continuity that it suggests. The trap is in the verb *to be*, which, according to Schopenhauer, is merely the nexus that joins the subject and the predicate in every clause. But remove both terms and what remains is a baseless word, a sound.[6]

And speaking of objections, I want to contradict those that Spencer, in his illustrious *Principles of Psychology* (volume 2, page 505), voices in opposition to the doctrine of idealism. Spencer argues:

> Of the proposition that there is no existence beyond consciousness, the first implication is that consciousness is unlimited in extension. For a limit which consciousness cannot transcend, implies an existence which imposes the limit; and this must either be an existence beyond consciousness, which is contrary to

6 In the course on metaphysics conceived by José Campillo y Rodríguez, it is asserted that the axiomatic argument *cogito, ergo sum* is nothing more than an abbreviation of an idea that the physician from Medina, Gómez Pereira, published in 1554. A paraphrase of the early Castillian reads in the following way: *Nosco me aliquid noseere: at quidquid noscit, est: ergo ego sum.* I know that I know something and that everything that is known exists; therefore I am.

I have also read—in an old *Vie de Mounsier Descartes*, published in Paris in 1691 and of which I have only the second volume, mateless and missing the author's name—that many earnestly accused Descartes of having pilfered his speculation regarding the mechanical nature of animals from the book *Antoniana Margarita* by the aforementioned Gómez Pereira. This same book includes the above cited formulation.

> the hypothesis, or an existence within consciousness other than itself, which is also contrary to the hypothesis. Something which restrains consciousness to a certain sphere, whether it be internal or external, must be something other than consciousness—must be something co-existing, which is contrary to the hypothesis. Hence consciousness being unrestrained in its sphere becomes infinite in space.

The above contains various fallacies. To reason that if nothing exists beyond consciousness, the latter must be limitless is like arguing that I have infinite capital in my pocket since the entire thing is made up of pennies. *Nothing exists beyond consciousness* is the same as saying: Everything that happens is of a spiritual order; a matter of quality that doesn't affect in the least the quantity of events which line up in succession to form a life.

As for the concluding sentence, it is incomprehensible. Space, according to the idealists, does not exist in and of itself: it is a mental phenomenon, like pain, fear, and vision, and, being part of consciousness, it may in no way be said that consciousness is situated in space.

Spencer goes on:

> A further implication is that consciousness is infinite in time. To conceive any limit to consciousness in the past, is to conceive [either] that preceding this limit there was some other actual existence at the moment when consciousness commenced, which would be contrary to the hypothesis . . .

To which one may respond by pointing out that such infinity of time does not necessarily signify an extensive duration. Imagine, as do certain nonphilosophers, that all that exists is the subject and that everything that occurs is nothing but a vision unfurling from his spirit. Time would last exactly as long as the vision, which we have no trouble imagining as very brief. There would be no time before the beginning of the dream or after its end, since time is an intellectual construct and objectively does not exist. Thus we would have an eternity that would encompass all possible time and nevertheless fit into a few scant seconds. Also, the theologians would have had to translate the eternity of God into a duration without beginning or end, without vicissitudes or change, in a pure present.

Spencer concludes:

> In the absence of any other existence limiting it in time and space, consciousness must be absolute or unconditioned . . . Everything within it is self-determined . . . Hence, any state of consciousness, as a pain, is self-produced, and continues only in virtue of conditions which consciousness itself imposes. The ending of any state, say a pleasure, is caused solely by the operation of consciousness on itself . . .

The artifice of such argumentation rests on the fundamental, personal—we might almost say mythological—meaning that Spencer confers to the word *consciousness*, a wholly unjustifiable act . . .

And with this I rest my case. Concerning the negation of the autonomous existence of things both visible and palpable, it is easy to come to an agreement about it by thinking thus: Reality is like that image of ourselves that appears in every mirror, a simulacrum that exists because of us, that comes, gestures, and leaves with us, but that is always found, simply by looking for it.

[*1923*] [*SJL/JP*]

"THE TRAGIC EVERYDAY, THE BLIND PILOT, WORDS AND BLOOD"

If someone in this century is comparable to the Egyptian Proteus, that someone is Giovanni Papini, who once signed his name Gian Falco, literary historian and poet, pragmatist and romantic, atheist and later theologian. We don't know which face was his, because his masks were many. To speak of masks is perhaps an injustice. Papini, throughout his long life, could have sustained antagonistic doctrines with sincerity. (We are reminded, in passing, of Lugones's analogous destiny.) There are styles which do not allow their author to speak in discreet tones. In polemics Papini tended to be emphatic, indeed booming. He rejected the *Decameron* and rejected *Hamlet*.

He was born in Florence in 1881. According to his biographers, his origins were modest but having been born in Florence meant having inherited, beyond some dubious genealogical trees, an admirable secular tradition. He was a hedonistic reader, not pressured by exams, always moved to read for pleasure. The first object of his attention was philosophy. He translated and critiqued books by Bergson, Schopenhauer, and Berkeley. Schopenhauer speaks of the dreamlike essence of life, and for Berkeley, universal history is a long dream of God who creates and perceives it infinitely. Such concepts were not mere abstractions for Papini. In light of them he composed the stories that comprise this book, dating from the turn of the century.

In 1912 he published *The Twilight of the Philosophers*, a

title that's a variation on Nietzsche's *Twilight of the Idols*, a title that's a variation on "Twilight of the Gods" in the first poem of the *Elder Edda*. From idealism Papini switched to a pragmatism he defined as psychological and magical, and not quite the same as William James's. Years later he would invoke it to justify fascism. His melancholy autobiography *The Failure* (original: *Un uomo finito*) appeared in 1913. His most famous books (*Life of Christ, Gog, If Dante Were Alive, The Devil*) were written to be masterpieces, a genre which requires a certain innocence on the part of the author.

In 1921 he converted, not without some publicity, to the Catholic faith. He died in Florence in 1956.

I must have been ten years old when I read, in a bad Spanish translation, *The Tragic Everyday* and *The Blind Pilot*. Other readings erased them. Without realizing, I acted wisely: forgetting can be a profound form of memory. Around 1969 I composed in Cambridge the fantastic story "The Other." Astonished and grateful, I realize now that this story repeats the plot of a fable by Papini called "Two Images in a Pond."

[*1985*] [*SJL*]

DO YOU BELIEVE IN GOD?

Interview with Borges

Do you believe in God?

If by God we imply a single personality or a trinity, some sort of supernatural man, a judge of our actions and thoughts, I don't believe in that being. On the other hand, if by God we mean a moral or mental purpose in the universe, I certainly believe in Him. Regarding the problem of personal immortality, which Unamuno and other writers have connected to the notion of God, I don't believe in it, nor do I desire to be personally immortal.

That there is an order in the universe, a system of periodic recurrences and a general evolution, seems to me obvious. No less undeniable to me is the existence of a moral law, of an intimate feeling of having acted well or badly in each occasion.

Do you mean, essentially, that all this would prove the existence of God, or that he has been the creator, the beginning and end of everything?

I don't know if God is in the beginning of the cosmic process, but possibly he's at the end. God is perhaps an aspiration toward which the universe is predisposed.

And why do you believe in God in this way?

I believe intuitively and, besides, it would be despairing not to believe. If we presume there is a perfect and omnipotent being at the beginning of universal history, and we presume also that he created the world, then we cannot understand why pain and evil exist. If we assume, on the other hand, a God who is in the process of creation as the cosmos or our individual destiny evolves, in that particular form we can believe in Him, that is, as an evolving passage toward perfectibility.

And how do you apply your belief to the practices of everyday life?

I try to apply it. Within the constraints of the life to which I am conditioned, I do the best I can. Besides, I do not demand of my ambition's limits more than what the natural process of my own evolution can give me. I try to be a good man, but I don't always succeed.

[1956] *[SJL]*

Sources

"The Circular Ruins"
"Las ruinas circulares"; reprinted from *Collected Fictions*; originally published in *Fictions*, "The Garden of Forking Paths" (1941).

"The Library of Babel"
"La biblioteca de Badel"; reprinted from *Collected Fictions*; originally published in *Fictions*, "The Garden of Forking Paths" (1941).

"Funes the Memorious"
"Funes el memorioso"; reprinted from *Collected Fictions*; originally published in *Fictions*, "Artifices" (1944).

"The Aleph"
"El Aleph"; reprinted from *Collected Fictions*; originally published in *The Aleph* (1949).

"The Zahir"
"El Zahir"; reprinted from *Collected Fictions*; originally published in *The Aleph* (1949).

"The Writing of the God"
"La escritura del Dios"; reprinted from *Collected Fictions*; originally published in *The Aleph* (1949).

"The Simurgh and the Eagle"
"El Simurgh y el águila"; reprinted from *Selected Non-Fictions*; originally published in *La Nación* (1948).

"A New Refutation of Time"
"Nueva refutación del tiempo"; reprinted from *Selected Non-Fictions;* originally published in *Otras inquisiciones* (1952).

"Paradiso XXXI, 108"
"Paradiso XXXI, 108"; reprinted from *Selected Poems*; originally published in *The Maker* (1960).

"Epilogue to *Dreamtigers*"
"Epílogo"; reprinted from *Selected Poems*; originally published in *The Maker* (1960).

"Poem of the Gifts"
"Poema de los dones"; reprinted from *Selected Poems;* originally published in *Poems* (1959).

"Matthew XXV: 30"
"Mateo, XXV, 30"; reprinted from *Selected Poems*; originally published in *The Self and the Other* (1964).

"On Salvation by Deeds"
"De la salvación por las obras"; reprinted from *Atlas;* originally published in *Atlas* (1984).

"Patio"
"Patio"; reprinted from *Selected Poems*; originally published as "Un Patio" in *Fervor de Buenos Aires* (1923).

"George Santayana"
"George Santayana"; new translation; "biografía sintética" (capsule biography) originally published in *Home* (1937).

"Thomas Mann on Schopenhauer"
"Un libro de Thomas Mann sobre Schopenhauer"; new translation; a review originally published in *Home* (1939).

"Berkeley's Crossroads"
"La encrucijada de Berkeley"; new translation; originally published in *Nosotros* (1923) and included in *Inquisiciones* (1925).

"The Tragic Everyday, The Blind Pilot, Words and Blood"
"Lo tragico cotidiano, El piloto ciego, Palabra y sangre"; new translation; Prologue published in *Biblioteca personal* (1985).

"Do You Believe in God?"
"¿Cree Usted en Dios?"; new translation; source published in *Textos recobrados* (1956); originally published in *Mundo Argentino*.

Printed in the United States
by Baker & Taylor Publisher Services